MW00887252

THE TRUTH IS A LIE

The complete psychological and mo-
tivational journey to personal trans-
formation through conscience
thought, relationship analysis and
educational conditioning.

Harry Petsanis

What is right is not always popular, and what is popular is not always right.

—ALBERT EINSTEIN

To all of the people who have given me so much, to whom I have given so little. I dedicate the rest of my life to reversing that trend. Special thanks to Tiffany Abbott whose hard work and dedication made this book possible.
-Harry Petsanis

INTRODUCTION

In *The Wizard of Oz*, Dorothy, the Cowardly Lion, the Scarecrow, and the Tin Man learn that the wizard behind the curtain is controlling all the myth and magic in Oz. The wizard does not want to be revealed. He wants to stay in control, and for the illusion of a perfect and harmonious world to continue. Follow my journey in *The Truth is a Lie* as I pull back the curtain and show that your Land of Oz is a place where your perception is not reality.

Every day we live in conflict. We say that we want the curtain pulled back to reveal the truth, but our nature prefers to keep us in the dark, not allowing us to see who we truly are. In many instances, we simultaneously fear and despise the person we know is directly behind that lightly threaded fabric. We want nothing to do with the truth because the lie that we have been living for so long has become our reality. Imagine a wrecking ball destroying the infrastructure of all that we have been manipulated to believe. This Land of Oz was created by those in power: the government, educators, parents, and authority figures to control society and manipulate the minds of the less fortunate and powerless to create the illusion of a perfect world, and more importantly, protect the lives of those controlling us. Imagine a boxer, as soon as the bell rings, coming at you. He hits you with a haymaker to knock you off balance. As soon as we are born, our bell rings, and we are hit with the reality of the world that has already been created for us. The Land of Oz that has been created for you has your own wizard pulling the strings and brainwashing you to believe only what they want you to believe.

People need to be shaken in a dramatic fashion to get them out of their conditioned apathy. We are so entrenched in the way we think that only a catastrophic event or soulfully truthful revelation can rewire the hardware. This conditioning has internally and emotionally tied us up in knots. We're afraid to reveal ourselves to people, afraid to speak out or to act in a way that truly reflects how we think and feel, and we're afraid to admit that at heart we are all self-serving and self-indulgent beings. Even Mother Teresa acknowledged that she felt guilty about how good it made her feel to help other people. This fear has been ingrained in us, causing us to lead the life that others demand of us, which was their intention from the beginning. Throughout our journey, my goal will be to get you to pull back the curtain in your Land of Oz and reveal your world as it really is, not as you and others have conditioned you to believe that it is.

CONTENTS

Dedication   1

Introduction   2

Chapter 1: Personal Agendas   7

Chapter 2: Selfishness   10

Chapter 3: The Ripple-in-the-Pond Theory   12

Chapter 4: The Sherlock Holmes Theory   14

Chapter 5: Motive   17

Chapter 6: Home Lessons: Who Really Benefits?   23

Chapter 7: Education: Nothing Changes   26

Chapter 8: Bullying   29

Chapter 9: Bizarro World   32

Chapter 10: The Problem Within   35

Chapter 11: The Formative Years   38

Chapter 12: Relationships   41

Chapter 13: The Purpose of Communication   44

Chapter 14: The Most Dishonest form of Communication   47

Chapter 15: Positions of Power   51

Chapter 16: The Family Dynamic   53

Chapter 17: Youth is Wasted on the Young   55

Chapter 18: Behavior Modification   57

Chapter 19: The Dangers of Conformity   60

Chapter 20: Religion is Above Reproach   63

Chapter 21: Human Nature   67

Chapter 22: Beliefs and Opinions   71

Chapter 23: Internal and External Conflicts   74

Chapter 24: Inconsistency in Humans   78

Chapter 25: Perceptions   81

Chapter 26: Drugs and Laws   84

Chapter 27: The Price of Profit   88

Chapter 28: Hiding Behind our Masks   91

Chapter 29: People's Disposition is Determined by Their Position   94

Chapter 30: Accountability   98

Chapter 31: Societal Versus Personal Accountability   102

Chapter 32: The Name Game   105

Chapter 33: Fraud   108

Chapter 34: Do as I Say, Not as I Do   110

Chapter 35: Flip the Script   113

Epilogue   117

Bibliography   118

CHAPTER ONE

Personal Agendas

Everyone has an agenda. The minute someone tells me they don't is the second I know they do. Agendas can produce positive results, but they often come from our self-serving nature. For example, a billionaire gives millions of dollars to charity for the sole purpose of a tax write-off. The billionaire's driving desire is to save on his taxes. The result is that a charity and thousands of people benefit. The mistake we make is never ascertaining someone's agenda and never acknowledging that we have one. Once it is ascertained, an honest conversation can occur.

Conflict happens when someone else's agenda doesn't align with our own. This conflict is often to our own detriment. Adults and authority figures have an agenda, often using it to suppress and control children to make their own lives easier. This tendency may be subconscious, but that doesn't minimize the effect it has on children who are powerless to overcome it.

For a primary example: Education. Teachers no longer interact and teach to elevate the knowledge of children; they teach to elevate test scores. Increasing students' test scores is mandated by a scholastic focus on analytics and scores instead of education and knowledge. This mandated criterion is based on funding, not education. Teachers acquiesce to administrators, administrators acquiesce to regional superintendents, regional superintendents acquiesce to chief officers, chief officers acquiesce to head superintendents, head superintendents acquiesce to the school board. All acquiesce to the agenda of the Department of Education.

Agendas are rooted in extraction. This extraction is emotional, psychological, and often financial. When determining someone's agenda simply conclude what they are trying to extract; like bread crumbs on a trail, it will lead you to their driving force.

Example #2: Financial agenda
- Black Friday. Black Friday has become an unofficial holiday in the United States. It is the continued indulgence of Thanksgiving. Companies represent monumental discounts to induce customers to frequent their businesses on Thanksgiving evening, Black Friday, and Cyber Monday. These companies create a façade that convinces society that the sales they are promoting are for the consumers' benefit, causing millions of customers to flock to their establishments. The motivation behind this façade is to turn these companies' books from red to black while turning customers' bank accounts from black to red. Black Friday was created to allow businesses to overcome their own mismanagement. Strong marketing and a misrepresented societal agenda allow them to accomplish this in only three days.

Example #3: Emotional agenda:
- Whenever my opinion differed from my parents, they would say things that hurt me. Children are not emotionally or psychologically evolved to withstand personal attacks. I didn't realize until later that this was my parents' tactic. My parents knew that

hurting me would stop me in my tracks, allowing them to pursue their agenda, which was to remove me from the equation and fill their free time with whatever interested them.

Example #4: Psychological agenda:

- Psychologically, I learned to use my parents' emotional agenda to my benefit. Once I realized that getting me out of their hair was their priority, I would extort my mother financially for it. When I felt emotionally attacked, I feigned that it caused me pain. The following day, I would tell my mother how hurtful their words were. I knew this would psychologically work to my benefit, causing her to financially compensate me to ease my discomfort. My mother could have eased my pain in a more productive and psychologically beneficial way, but that was something that neither of us desired. Once I understood that their goal was to eliminate me from the equation, I decided to eliminate them from my equation. Their agenda was to minimize their interaction with me, and my agenda became to maximize revenue, creating a very destructive and emotionally disconnected relationship between my parents and myself.

Lesson learned: An agenda is like a game of dominoes. Once it's ascertained, all that needs to be done is to put the slightest pressure on the first domino, and then sit back and watch every domino topple.

CHAPTER TWO

Selfishness

The most misrepresented word in society is *selfish*. Everyone is selfish, but this label is mostly used when one person's agenda supersedes another's. The definition of selfish is "concerned excessively and exclusively with oneself" (*Merriam-Webster*.com). The irony is the people attaching this label to you are upset that you won't prioritize their needs above yours. Once this occurs, guilt, manipulation, coercion, and bullying come into play.

Selfishness and human nature are synonymous: you can't have one without the other. The definition of selfish has never changed, what's changed is society's perception of the word. Once people realized they could manipulate the word to attain their desires, the stigma was created.

Example: When I was ten or eleven, I went to a funeral with my family. This was a funeral for someone that my parents knew from church. After the service, I told my parents that I could not understand why everyone was sad and crying. My parents said it was because the person who had passed away was a good person and that he was beloved. I told my parents that their answer contradicted everything that I heard people discussing at the service and all that I had been taught to believe. I explained that I overheard people saying the man was no longer suffering and was in a better place. If what they were saying was accurate, and he was in a better place, then why would they feel the need to cry? My parents then asked me why I thought everyone was crying. Before I answered, I inherently knew two things: I would be taken to the woodshed for telling them the truth, and the only reason they asked for my opinion was to deflect the fact that they did not have an answer to my question. I told my parents they were crying because they were selfish. If it truly was about the man being in a better place, then they should be smiling, laughing, and rejoicing. But since everyone's behavior was to the contrary, it showed me that it had nothing to do with the deceased and was simply people conveying and expressing their own selfish feelings to others who felt the exact same way. From that experience, I learned that if people allow their selfish nature and personal agendas to supersede death, then it's always going to take priority in life. I also found the event to be hypocritical, telling my parents that the church's teachings of heaven should have had all the people celebrating since the man would be in a better place, which had always been expressed to me as nirvana.

I learned three valuable lessons that day. First, people's personal agendas and selfish perspectives often supersede an event or the greater good. Second, what we're taught often comes into direct conflict with what we experience. When we are taught something it's often done to make someone else's life easier, not because it's true. Third, when people ask you for the truth, they truly want to hear the lie that they have already formulated in their own minds. If your truth doesn't match their lie, they selfishly realize that an investment of their time must occur.

CHAPTER THREE

The Ripple-in-the-Pond Theory

L ife's events can be likened to ripples in a pond. When the first rip-
ple occurs, it sets off a chain reaction that leads to larger, more momentous ripples, eventually creating a tsunami. This concept also applies to people's behavior. When someone's initial action, motive, thought, or agenda is revealed, every subsequent action, motive, thought, or agenda can be predicted.

Example: After the signing of the Declaration of Independence, political factions began to form. Initially, the Founding Fathers opposed the divisive nature of a political system, knowing it would be societal suicide. This was the first ripple in the pond. Those same politicians who opposed a division of the political system allowed their egos and personal agendas to override their political acumen. That was the second ripple. The political system that those politicians detested, but allowed to be implemented, was already contradicting the Constitution they had created. That was ripple number three. George Washington, America's first president, never wanted the position. He accepted the presidency to unify a country that was already splitting at the seams from the implementation of a volcanic political structure. That was ripple number four.

Ripple number five: today's political and societal climate is toxic. The creation of political parties was meant to give everyone a voice. The politicians who created the division failed to factor in human nature. The intent may have been to give everyone a voice, but the reality became complete chaos. We are no longer a society that accepts losing an election to someone who doesn't match our agenda. People would rather see the country fail than not have their personal agendas fulfilled. Ripple number six: our country has never been more divided.

Lesson learned: The ripple-in-the-pond theory is simplistic. The mistake that many people make when casting the first stone is refusing to have the foresight that once the stone is cast, subsequent ripples cannot be controlled.

Harry Petsanis

CHAPTER FOUR

The Sherlock Holmes Theory

In 1887, Sherlock Holmes came to life. Sir Arthur Conan Doyle modeled the character of Holmes on his professor from the University of Edinburgh Medical School, Dr. Joseph Bell. Bell's method of diagnosis was used in "Holmes's uncanny ability to gather evidence based upon his honed skills of observation and deductive reasoning" (*Encyclopedia Britannica, Inc*). Doyle theorized through Holmes, proclaiming that, "When you have excluded the impossible, whatever remains, however improbable, must be the truth" (*Encyclopedia Britannica, Inc*).

Sherlock Holmes would look at each intricate detail, analyze every discernible clue, and then draw his conclusion based on facts, not theories or agendas. If society subscribed to this technique, the world would be a more logical place. Sadly, society doesn't subscribe to the Sherlock Holmes Theory, it subscribes to the Sherlock Holmes Theory in reverse. Society draws their conclusions first, then manipulates every fact, piece of evidence, statement, and odds of probability to fit their pre-determined narrative.

Example: America considers itself to be the land of democracy, and it may be now, but it didn't begin that way. America was stolen from the original and rightful owners, the Native Americans. Immediately, our forefathers changed that narrative, and then every fact, clue, and piece of evidence was twisted to paint America in the light that it demanded to be seen in. Already "the game was afoot" and the Sherlock Holmes Theory in reverse was being undertaken. Once the *Americanized* narrative was created, every subsequent action reinforced the original misrepresentation. As a journalism major, I was required to take courses in history. Kindergarten through college equated to over twenty years of my life. For approximately fifteen of those years, I wasn't taught history, I was taught "American History." Not once in those "American History" books do I recall reading about the genocide of multiple tribes of Native Americans. Millions, if not billions, of dollars, have been spent to reinforce the narrative that was created hundreds of years ago. Many people would believe that money to be well spent, refusing to accept and acknowledge the reality of America's origin.

Example #2: Love. The definition of love is "warm attachment, enthusiasm, or devotion for another." In America, the standard classroom dictionary is the Merriam-Webster Dictionary, which was created in 1828. Webster's definition of love has become universally accepted. This is another example of the Sherlock Holmes Theory in reverse. In my opinion, love is one of life's most selfish emotions. We don't love someone or feel great affection for them based on who they are, we love someone and feel great affection for them based on who we are. It isn't that someone is exciting, it's that we feel excited. They're not interesting, we find them interesting. We don't see them as attractive, they're attractive to us. The feelings that we have aren't about someone else, they're about us. This narrative was changed to create an illusion that could be monetized: Valentine's Day, Mother's Day, Father's Day, Christmas Day, are all based around the illusion of loving someone or something, and that illusion is rooted in the changed narrative.

Lesson learned: All that's required to have a changed narrative accepted is power, money, and time. The changing of a narrative is equivalent to planting a tree: find fertile soil, create a foundation, plant the seed, entrench it, water it, and watch it grow.

CHAPTER FIVE

Motive

The word "agenda" has been used many times; another word that expresses the same sentiment is motive. Every time we watch a movie that's a courtroom drama, the focus is on the defendant's motive for the alleged crime. I find it perplexing that the legal system prioritizes motive to determine a defendant's punishment, but as a society, we pay no attention to someone's motive when we are personally doling out punishment. Everyone has a motive. When someone's motive is revealed, this allows us to accurately assess the level of punishment or blame that we want to attribute to their behavior. In a utopian environment, the motive would be for our actions to reflect who we really are and to be comfortable with ourselves. In a realistic environment, acting in a way that's truly reflective of what we think and feel, won't often attain the results we're seeking from others, causing our motive to shift from mindful to manipulative.

It isn't just important for us to focus on others' motives; it's equally important to focus on our own. The reason we do not focus on our own motives is that we do not want to see ourselves as disingenuous and conniving. We rarely see someone else's motive, but when it comes to our own, we are legally blind. The more our motive reveals itself, the more we turn from it. When we want something from someone, we do not want to look at the motive behind our action, because if we look at the motive, it often detours our action.

Parents often teach children to question everyone else's motives. The one thing that parents omit, when they tell us to question everyone and everything, is that they never want us to question them. Every time my dad asked me to do something, I would ask why, and his reply was always the same, "Because I told you to," or that it was what he was taught to do. When I would question him further, he would become defensive and angry and took my questioning as me challenging him. I was just doing what he taught me, never realizing he wasn't consistent in his teaching. Initially, this conflict was confusing, but eventually, it proved invaluable. In another circumstance where I questioned my dad, he asked why I had to question everything and everyone and where did that come from? When I replied that it came from him, he said, "You never got that from me." I responded by saying, "Weren't you the one who told me to question everyone and everything, especially people's motives?" Before he could reply, he started laughing and then I said, "What's so funny?" he replied, "I'm not used to you paying attention to me." Even though my dad never verbally acknowledged that I was correct, his laughter spoke volumes. Although my dad laughed, I knew he still didn't like the fact that I questioned him and didn't want me doing it in the future. These early examples of hypocrisy were difficult, but they had long-lasting psychological benefits. My dad's response was not unique to him, it was behavior that I still encounter to this day.

People say that we should trust others until they give us a reason not to trust them. If this was true, there would be no need to question everyone and everything. Before trust, respect, love, or any other emotion or characteristic can be determined, motive must be uncovered and examined. The motive is often revealed when we question someone's intent. Do I enter any situation trusting just anyone? Never. Does that mean that I do not trust people initially? Of course. As a society, we do not trust people despite saying that we do. We say that we trust people until they give us a reason not to, or that we respect people, even if they don't respect us. These comments appear genuine on the surface, but they are disingenuous at their base.

Example #1: We lock our vehicles, put our money in banks, have security systems in our homes, businesses, and automobiles. All these actions show what we really believe others' motives to be. It is dangerous to show society any vulnerability until we have determined what their motive is. Our behavior proves that we do not trust people. As previously stated, we lock our doors, our vehicles, and our businesses, we clutch our purses tightly, and we secure our money and our valuables, and those behaviors are not only not wrong, they are logical when accurately assessing the motives of a society that potentially intends to do us harm. Once motive is ascertained, short and long-term damage can often be avoided.

Example #2: When I bought my fitness center, I purchased new equipment, and financed it through a nationally accredited bank. Four or five months into my payments, I received a call from a bank representative, asking if I would be interested in paying off the loan early. He represented that the call was to benefit me when the motive was solely to benefit the bank, who was trying to accumulate cash quickly. I knew I could benefit from them being in a get-cash-now mode. I told them that if they needed money quickly to make me an enticing offer and that I would think about it. The representative immediately changed his approach and asked me what I had in mind. At that point, I owed $25,000 for the equipment. I suggested they cut the balance in half and I would pay it off in two payments. He put me on hold and came back saying they could take off $2,000. I said I was not interested. After 20 minutes of haggling, they said they could knock $7,000 off the balance, but would not do one penny more. I accepted the offer and changed the payoff from two months to four. After agreeing to the terms, he told me he would overnight me the paperwork and once it was signed and returned, I would be released from my original contract. The original contract had a provision stipulating that if I was late on one payment, the entire balance could be called due. I told him that being released from the original agreement was an absolute necessity. He told me he was going to handle it personally and he would be sending me the paperwork to sign to terminate the original agreement. He added that the call was being recorded to assure me there would be no mistakes. I replied that I was also recording the call, which he never contested. After signing the new agreement, which simultaneously released me from the old one, I made my first payment of $4,450. Approximately one month later, and one day before my second payment was due, I received a package from the bank stating that I had missed my monthly payment and demanding the entire balance be paid. I called the representative, who informed me that it was his mistake, that he forgot to file the paperwork with the proper department to release me from the prior agreement, and that he would handle it and call me back within the hour. Two hours later, he informed me that they would release me from the original contract once I had made my last payment.

The motive from the bank shifted from getting my money to extorting me for their mistake. I told him I would call him back within the hour. I contacted my attorney, who also happened to be a member of my gym and brought him up to speed. The next day he informed me that a civil lawsuit had been filed against me and my company, demanding the entire balance be paid. I was upset until he told me this was the best thing that could've happened. He said the lawsuit opened the door for a counter-suit for breach of contract, fraud, and inducement to enter into a contract. He told me not to speak to anyone, and to pull my credit reports, explaining that if they considered me thirty days past due on a payment and filed with the local small claims division, there was a very good chance they reported me and my company to all three credit bureaus, which they had. My lawyer filed a counter-suit and within two months we were meeting with a mediator. He laid out our case, presenting both contracts, showing opposing counsel the clause in the second one, which immediately terminated the first one. He pulled out his tape recorder and played all the conversations I had with their bank's representative. Opposing counsel objected to the recordings, and my attorney responded by reminding them that there are no objections during mediation and their representative signed off on my recording of the conversations.

Opposing counsel knew from the agreements that I had been released, and they heard from the recordings that I had been extorted. Shifting gears, opposing counsel's onus changed from my lack of payment to the assertion that I hadn't been damaged by their mistake. Their motive was no different than the motive of the representative: it was to avoid accountability and shift responsibility. My attorney stated that the filing of a lawsuit created a public record that did insurmountable damage to my personal and business reputation. This fact was indisputable. After opposing counsel had a session in private with the mediator, they acknowledged that filing the claim did damage my reputation, but said it was difficult to put a monetary value on a public filing. My attorney asked for a private session in counsel with his client (me). During this session, he told me to keep my mouth shut and that we had them right where we wanted them. When we reentered mediation, my attorney asked opposing counsel what they considered to be damaging. The banks' lawyer replied that any personal affidavit regarding the public filing or alteration to a credit score would be considered damaging. My attorney handed them my six credit reports: three reports dated one month before the lawsuit and three reports dated one month after. All three credit reports from after the filing showed a drop in my credit score, directly related to the lawsuit. At that point, the damage could no longer be refuted.

Their motive was to minimize damage. Knowing that would be their motive going in, our motive was to use their motive against them. Having leverage, there was no need for us to negotiate. We left the meeting with a signed agreement that all three credit bureaus would be informed of the banks' mistake and that my credit scores would be returned to their previous numbers. The first payment of $4,450 would be reimbursed to me, no subsequent payments from me would be required, the entire balance on the note for my equipment would be eliminated, and a $20,000 payment would be made to me based on the damage that they had done and the lack of accountability they demonstrated.

Lesson learned: When you understand someone's motive and their intent, you immediately understand the position they've taken and, more importantly, the position they're trying to put you in. Never rush when ascertaining someone's motive. Once you've taken that necessary time to fully understand someone's motive, you've gone from the inferior position to the superior one.

CHAPTER SIX

Home Lessons: Who Really Benefits?

Adults believe what they teach children is for the child's benefit. This deception is a form of control and occurs in every family. Our parents' teachings may often benefit us, but they always benefit them. We are in a completely vulnerable position as children, empowering the person or people who are suppressing us and forcing us to modify our behavior. Adults are aware of the power they have over children and, consciously or subconsciously, they are aware of children's position of inferiority. Because children are in an inferior position, they are helpless to fight the power that parents and adults have over them.

Example: I was always starving when I would come home from school. The minute I went to the refrigerator, I was admonished by my mother. She would always say, "We don't eat until your dad gets home." When I asked why she would say that it was important that we eat as a family and that I needed to honor my dad's wishes. I replied, "Why should I have to wait for someone else when I'm hungry now?" My mother answered by saying that when I was grown up and owned my own home, I could eat whenever I wanted. Upset because my mother knew I couldn't change my age or circumstance, I replied, "If dad truly valued having dinner with us, then he wouldn't spend the entire meal watching television."

This shaped my instincts on human nature. My eating before dinner had nothing to do with me, our family's eating habits, or my dad spending quality time with us, it was simply a way for my parents to exercise control over me and force me to bend to their will, knowing I was not capable of changing the rules being enforced upon me. It also showed the length they would go to maintain control over me. The initial representation my mother made is that I needed to honor my dad and that we needed to eat as a family. When my mother gave me this edict, I realized that she and my dad were not working in unison. My mother wasn't following my dad's edicts because she believed or agreed with them, she was in fear of the repercussions that would come from diso-beying them. By understanding my parent's behavior, I was able to un-derstand them. My dad wanted to control everyone and everything be-neath him. My mother wanted to avoid reprisal. Their thought process may have been illogical, but I was powerless to circumvent it. I realized that any legitimate point that I could convey would be shot down by my parent's position in the household. At that point, taking any conversa-tion to an elevated level became pointless and counterproductive.

The lesson learned was like the one from the funeral of my par-ent's friend: people's personal agendas will always trump logic, reason, and circumstance. My parent's self-benefit always superseded mine, giving me great insight into the adult-child dynamic.

Initially, this revelation was all-consuming and suffocating. We want to see our parents and people in our household through rose-col-ored glasses, not as human beings who have flaws and weaknesses. See-ing my parents for who they were caused a loss of innocence and

emotional disconnect within me, while at the same time laying a foundation of logic that fuels my thought process today.

Additional lesson learned: never assume that because someone is
close to you, in proximity, relation, or emotional attachment, that they
prioritize your interest or your reality over their interest or reality. Society has conditioned us to assume the closer someone is to us, the more
they prioritize our well-being over their own. Reality teaches us, the
closer someone is to us, the more they try to control and manipulate us.

CHAPTER SEVEN

Education: Nothing Changes

Growing up, our time is divided between home and school. Our time is split between being controlled by parents and teachers. My experience with school was not rooted in the things that I was taught, but in the way that I was controlled and suppressed. Control is an underlying theme throughout this book. Another is understanding the people who exercise control over us and why they do it. Teachers, like parents, often exercise control over children because they can't control any other facet of their lives. Teachers exert control through education the same way they are controlled outside of the classroom.

Teachers mandate where to sit, when we can eat, when we can use the bathroom, and where we stand in line. These repetitive suppressions start from day one, becoming part of our psychological and emotional DNA, forcing us down the path of conformity and complacency. These suppressions have nothing to do with teaching or educating, they have everything to do with creating an environment that makes the teachers surroundings more comfortable and tolerable.

Example: In elementary school, I was a smart-ass, always had a big mouth, and loved entertaining. Growing up in the '70s, report cards were hand-written, had to be taken home by the students, signed by their parents, and brought back to the teacher. Report cards had a section for additional notes and comments by the teacher. I never received a report card where every millimeter of space in the note section wasn't utilized. Every report card commented on me being a class clown, class disruptor, and distracting to the point where it made the teacher's job more difficult. These comments were written with a tone of cynicism and derision with the intent of my parents reading it that way, which they did. I was punished by my teachers and parents simply because I made their jobs more difficult. My sense of humor was a gift. Sadly, my parents and teachers chose to suppress my gift. The minute people decide you're making their life more difficult, the focus is no longer on the potential talent they may be witnessing, it's on eliminating the potential challenge that comes with it. This is the ultimate form of control. I was being punished for something I knew was one of my best attributes, which greatly diminished my self-worth. Imagine how many students' talents, dreams, and desires are extinguished simply because they make a teachers' job more difficult. If children are punished for showing the best of themselves, then what's left for them to show?

I graduated from the University of Akron with a degree in Mass Media Communications (Journalism). The university had a system in place that allowed students to drop classes until the last three days of the semester, with the professor's approved signature. When I asked my academic advisor how this could occur, she defended the university by explaining that they did not want to punish and dissuade students from proceeding towards their education, and a degree, by dampening their enthusiasm with failing grades. I perceived her answer to be disingenuous. I didn't respond, which caused her to ask me what I thought. I told her it was merely an issue of dollars and sense. If students weren't allowed to drop classes, then the likelihood of them dropping out of school and never returning would rise astronomically. By allowing students to drop classes up until the last three days of a semester, the university would not negatively affect their academic standing, which would increase their chances of staying in school, increasing the university's chances of monetarily benefiting from these students. I added that even though a high percentage of these students would eventually drop out, it would allow the university to get a few extra semesters of revenue out of them before they quit, culminating in hundreds of thousands of dollars in revenue per year.

Electives are another way that colleges bleed their students dry. Electives are the classes that colleges require their students to take, even though they have nothing to do with the student's major. These classes make up half the credits of graduating seniors and result in millions of dollars of revenue to the university, all under the guise of making a college student more well-rounded and enhancing their educational experience.

Example: math, science, history, and biology have nothing to do with the field of journalism, but I was required to take these courses, spend thousands of dollars on them, and I have not used any of these electives since the day I graduated. These electives had nothing to do with my degree and everything to do with monetizing me. Financial extortion causes students to take high-interest loans that take years, if not decades, to repay.

Lessons learned. Education has become big business. Its main designation is to monetarily extract from the students it professes to be educating. An education isn't something that people strive for, it's something that society is telling them they must acquire. This acquisition comes with an extremely high price tag which is determined by economists, not educators.

CHAPTER EIGHT

Bullying

Bullying has become one of the most controversial and pertinent issues in society. According to Webster's Dictionary, the definition of bullying is: "one who hurts or intimidates others." Many parents and teachers have mastered the art of bullying. Their constant need to control and modify children's behavior is the textbook definition of intimidation, which is the ultimate form of psychological bullying.

Psychological bullying appears in many forms, and in words such as: 'sit here,' 'do this,' 'eat now,' 'go to bed,' 'be quiet,' 'shut up,' 'don't interrupt,' and 'do what I say.' These statements and the behavior of parents and teachers have never been perceived as bullying, but they are at their genesis. As adults, it's difficult for us to break out of this suppressive strangle-hold, even when the bully is no longer present.

The description my parents gave me of a bully was someone who exerts their authority or power over someone else against their will, knowing that the other person does not have the ability to fight back or defend themselves. People who are in a superior position exercise power and authority daily. Parents can describe in detail what a bully is, but they're oblivious to the fact that they are often describing themselves.

Parents can exercise control judicially or for their own benefit. Sadly, they often choose the latter. The child is the one who suffers when the parent or teacher make the selfish choice. In many cases, the beating is emotional and psychological, not physical. The scars from these emotional and psychological beatings are not externally evident, but internally they run deep. Teen suicide rates are the second highest in the nation, which I mainly attribute to bullying in our society. (Population Reference Bureau, 2018).

In college, I would converse with a faculty member in the Psychology Department. Bullying was a topic we discussed. I told him the bullying children endure reminded me of a boxing match. When he asked me why I said because the inferior opponent (children) usually gets beaten into submission. He told me my analogy was missing two key components: the first being, in a boxing match, there are 15 rounds, and after each round, a boxer goes to his corner, regroups physically and emotionally, and discusses strategy with his manager. The second component was that in a boxing match, there's a referee whose sole job is to protect both fighters and stop the fight if it becomes one-sided. In life, these options do not exist.

He asked me if I was comfortable giving personal examples. I replied that when I was young, adults would ask me for my opinion. I *believed* they were doing it because they genuinely cared about me; therefore, they truly wanted to hear what I had to say. It wasn't until later that I realized this was a form of bullying. Every time my opinion differed from theirs, I was punished for it. He interjected, telling me this was a common societal dynamic. Many adults are unhappy with the choices they've made and the way their lives have turned out. Based on these poor choices, they are looking for someone or something to unleash their frustration on, and usually that someone is a defenseless child. Adults will ask a child a question, then use the child's answer as an opening to unleash the beast within. He told me that is the essence of bullying. His explanation made me see the parallel between families and war. In war, one side will probe and look for the weakness in their opponent's defense. Once they understand that weakness, then all they need is the slightest opening to attack. It's the same with adults: they ask children questions and then use their answers to attack, the only difference being, they are attacking because of their own weakness. We become immune to these behaviors because they occur at such an alarming rate that they become part of our emotional and psychological DNA.

Lesson learned: Bullying is a vicious cycle. We are bullied from the day we are born, not in the way that society perceives bullying, but in a way that is just as detrimental. We're caught off-guard by not expecting the attack to come from the people who should be protecting us. These people are the proverbial wolf in sheep's clothing. We were conditioned to believe that the adult figures in our life always have our best interests at heart. Once we realize that statement to be erroneous, the wolf is already devouring us, extracting its pound of flesh. Again, this devouring is often emotional and psychological, not physical. We are told that "sticks and stones may break our bones, but words will never hurt us." I've always considered this the stupidest and most ridiculous cliché. I can't recall anyone describing abuse in their childhood where psychological abuse was less devastating than the physical. A broken bone can heal within weeks or months, and doctors will tell you it can even heal stronger after a break. That's never the case with emotional abuse. We may recover from it, but it takes a lot longer, and rarely do we heal stronger.

CHAPTER NINE

Bizzaro World

Bizarro is a character and an enemy of Superman. In every way, Bizarro is the antithesis of Superman: his attire, thought process, the way he speaks, the way he acts, and how he processes information. His world is like the world that we were raised in and currently live in, the opposite of what we were told it was. We are taught that the world is like Superman: it's beautiful, flawless, and perfect. The world is anything but that, having all the attributes and characteristics that he personifies.

Examples:
- We are told that people are genuinely good and genuinely care. Our experiences show us they often don't.
- We are told that people are trustworthy and reliable. Our experience shows us that they often are not.
- We are told that we live in a democracy and that the government was instituted to protect us and have our best interest at heart. Experience shows us that couldn't be further from the truth. The government has their best interest at heart, and their only concern for us is how they can extort and monetize us.

- On the side of many police cars, we see the phrase "to protect and serve." Experience has taught us that that slogan should often read "to harass and extort."
- We are told that a doctor's main objective is the health and concern of their patients. Experience teaches us that their main concern is often to medicate and monetize us.
- We are told that people are honest and direct. Experience teaches us that people are often neither of those things.
- We are told that religion is meant to bring people together and to unify communities. History teaches us that war is often the by-product of religion and that more physical and emotional abuse has been caused and covered-up by religion than all other professions combined.
- Lawyers are often referred to as sharks, shysters, and con-men. My experience with lawyers is more positive than my experience with doctors.
- We are told that it is rude to interrupt and that when adults ask us a question, we are obligated to answer. I have every right to interrupt someone when they are invading my personal or emotional space and a person's age shouldn't obligate me to answer their question(s).
- We are told to respect authority figures. This undeserved and unearned respect has created a history of problems for society.
- We are told that it's poor manners not to ask people how they are or how they're doing. This has caused us to become a society that *says all the right words* without meaning or feeling behind them.
- We are told to preface and buffer our words when we are asking something of someone. This disingenuous prefacing and buffering has created an indirect society.

Life Lesson: This internal conflict was not something we were born with, it was drilled into us by people who wanted us to see the world through an idealist prism, and not as it really is. We are now faced with a moral dilemma: do we view society from the perspective of our teachings, or see society and people for who and what they really are?

CHAPTER TEN

The Problem Within

People despise confrontation, especially when it comes to confronting themselves. We should see every situation for what it is. If we do that, we will be able to ascertain its true meaning. Meaning and purpose are two words that are instrumental to personal growth, but with meaning and purpose comes conflict and discomfort.

Examples:
- Society has conditioned us that tipping is part of the foodservice industry. Our instincts tell us that we shouldn't be paying for someone else's employee.
- Society has conditioned us that if someone is in a position of need, we should help them. Instincts tell us to protect ourselves and not risk our personal safety.
- Society tells us to be who we are and say what we feel. Our instincts tell us that doing those two things come with great personal and professional ramifications.
- Society tells us that everyone should be treated equally. From the male perspective, this creates inner conflict because we are taught that it's our responsibility to make a woman happy.

Example: I love television and entertainment. The shows I watched growing up gave conflicting societal messages. Many of the issues regarding gender equality that exist today can be attributed to the misrepresentations and messages that have occurred throughout entertainment. "All in the Family," "Leave it to Beaver," "The Dick van Dyke Show," "The Donna Reed Show," "Cinderella," and "Snow White" were all shows and movies that portrayed males and females in very defined roles. Narrow-minded thinking like this forced the genders to contort their way of thinking to fit the roles that society enforced upon them. Women were supposed to be homemakers, raise the family, and attain self-worth through the happiness and achievement of others. Men were financially responsible for the entire family, defined by their professions, and expected to find fulfillment through their obligations. Gender-specification created a psychological and sociological division that has only widened.

The character Archie Bunker from "All in the Family" was a bigoted, ignorant, racist. He espoused opinions on every show and when his wife or son-in-law interjected, he verbally berated them by calling her "dingbat" and him "meathead." This conditioned men to believe that it was acceptable to suppress and verbally berate females and family members, while at the same time conditioning females that their opinion was less than valuable. Even when the behavior wasn't abusive, it was suppressive. "The Donna Reed Show," "The Dick van Dyke Show," and "Leave it to Beaver" all represented the perfect American family. The husband works, the wife is a homemaker, they live in suburbia in a beautiful home with the white picket fence and children in tow. These shows defined each gender's responsibility and obligation and showed society that the road to happiness only had one lane. This inner conflict can be linked to the beginning of the women's liberation movement and the sexual revolution.

"Cinderella" and "Snow White" did for the movies what these shows did for television. They showed men that their responsibility was to take a woman from her horrific surroundings and transport her to a life of excitement and enchantment. They showed women in vulnerable positions, waiting for someone or something to pull them out and they became dependent on a man for emotional satisfaction. The message conveying inner conflict goes beyond entertainment. Religious rituals prove this point.

Marriage should be the union of two equal parties moving forward in concert; instead, vows are exchanged where the words *cherish* and *obey* are uttered. Women are expected to take the man's name, immediately putting them in an inferior position. These roles are detrimental to both parties, forcing one party to be subservient and the other party to be responsible.

Lesson learned: When individuals, entertainment, and society pre-determine an individual's role, it creates inner conflict, causing individual and societal division. Many females, deservedly so, feel suppressed in being forced to define happiness as living for everyone else. Men are equally suppressed in having their happiness defined as being responsible, financially and emotionally, for the well-being of others.

CHAPTER ELEVEN

The Formative Years

The most important years are the formative years. They are also the most destructive. The old cliché is that "youth is wasted on the young." Children don't waste their youth; their youth is wasted by the people who control it. These years should be spent creating the foundation of the person we are going to be, not succumbing to the people who are creating us in their image. We are not psychologically, emotionally, or socially equipped to deal with many things at an early age. Since we are unequipped to deal with the most basic of things, we are easily manipulated, coerced, and controlled. The manipulation that occurs during our formative years causes a psychological imbalance in us that takes a lifetime to overcome.

A sponge's job is to soak up and absorb everything in its surroundings, and that's exactly what our brains and minds were meant to do. It's impossible for a sponge to absorb anything when it's already been filled to maximum density with someone else's ideas, thoughts, and opinions. People in a position of authority are threatened by another person's knowledge. The more educated one becomes, the more they question authority; the more they question authority, the more difficult it becomes for them to be controlled.

Once we realize that our teachings conflict with our experiences, a crack in our foundation is created. This crack often causes us to want to abandon, nurture and embrace nature. The minute we lean towards nature, is the minute the people controlling us yank us back to their path. This crack expands as we age, often causing our foundation to crumble. As children, we're not thinking about our foundation, we are focused on survival. We learn that questioning authority figures is often detrimental to us causing us to prioritize survival over our inquisitive nature. This conflict leads to a lifetime of avoiding punishment versus embracing happiness.

Example: I've never been religious. I believe there is a huge difference between religion and faith. Faith is one's personal belief. Religion is a business. I hated going to church and saw it for what I thought it was: a money-generating sham. My experience with the sermons in the Greek Orthodox church was that they were painfully long, which I felt was by design. During one of the services, they passed the collection plate around five times. I took this action as a personal affront. On the fifth passing of the plate, I took money out. This obviously created a problem for my parents, which created a problem for me. On the ride home, my dad was incensed. Before my dad could expound, I interjected that I despised going to church with every fiber of my being. This was one of the first times I truly stood my ground. I told him I thought it was nothing but a money-making scam and that I wasn't trying to change his opinion, but I didn't want to be bullied into going. I explained that the extortion that was occurring wasn't something I was comfortable with. I realized years later that my actions were nothing more than trying to get myself out of something that I was being forced to do. It's pathetic that we need to manipulate, lie, and go to such extreme measures simply because the direct approach doesn't work. At this point, I directed the conversation towards my mother. I told her that the length of the service had nothing to do with the message, it had everything to do with money. The longer the service, the more times the plate could be passed around.

The more times the plate could be passed around, the more revenue the church could generate. I also told her the church was using peer pressure to guilt their parishioners into donating, knowing they wouldn't want to look cheap in front of their friends and fellow attendees. If the church truly wanted to make it the person's choice, they would put the collection box in a location where people could privately give. We vote in private, we try clothes on in private, we have medical examinations in private, but we religiously donate in public, that's not unintentional. By the church making it public, they turn a donation into an obligation. To my mother's credit, she listened, which is vital for children in their formative years. I continued telling her that I also didn't understood why a church was called 'a house of God,' saying if it's God's house, then why are they always asking us to pay His bills? My dad interjected, telling me I was being sacrilegious. I said, "I'm not sacrilegious, I'm just asking a question. If it's His house, why are we paying His bills? Because He doesn't pay ours." To which my dad replied, "If you want to be accurate, you don't pay the bills at our house." Again, taking a position that I couldn't argue. I explained that I was paying with something a lot more valuable than his money: my time. I added that he was choosing to give his money to the church, and that I was being forced to give them my time and now I'm being punished for it. I knew I wasn't going to win this battle, but I was learning to find my own voice.

Lesson learned: This is a prime example of the sponge being filled by someone else. If I had been given the choice to fill my own sponge, I may have developed a much greater relationship with God and developed my faith to a higher level, but because my parents forced me into religion by compelling me to go to church and by filling every ounce of my sponge with their beliefs and agenda, there wasn't any space left in the sponge to fill with anything that pertained to me.

CHAPTER TWELVE

Relationships

Relationships are often connected by thread, not cable. A thread can be easily cut, and in a multitude of ways, severing the relationship. The reason our relationships with others are so difficult to maintain is that they're not relationships; they are connections based on mutual benefit, and the minute that one or both parties no longer perceive a mutual benefit, there is no longer a relationship. We do not value and appreciate other people for who they are, we value and appreciate how they benefit us. Take away the benefit and you take away the appreciation. It's a miracle that most *so-called* relationships last for any extended amount of time. The length of any relationship is directly tied to the length of your benefit to that person or their benefit to you.

What keeps a relationship going past the point of mutual benefit? There are a multitude of reasons people stay together: society's negative perception of divorce, insecurity, financial obligation, fear of physical and emotional reprisal, and pride are all at the top of my list. Staying in a relationship past the point of mutual benefit can be extremely detrimental to all involved.

Example #1: Marriage. The divorce rate is around 50%. Imagine what that percentage would be if people weren't obligated or contractually committed to staying together. When people allow themselves to be contractually bound to an emotional or personal commitment, irreparable harm to both parties can occur when feelings or emotions change. Commitment and affection turn into obligation, repulsion, and resentment. The one commonality that many marriages have is that the parties have nothing in common other than the fact that they feel obligated to stay together. A toxic environment is created for the people who remain married, their children, and their immediate family and friends, causing people to take sides, create alliances, hold grudges, and destroy families. Marriage is not the only relationship that's held together by a disingenuous thread.

Example #2: Religion. Idealistically, religion should be a person's relationship with a higher power and the church's role should be to facilitate that relationship. Realistically, the last thing the church wants to do is facilitate your relationship with a higher power, because the minute they do that, they can no longer facilitate a relationship with your pocketbook. Religion is the only business where we accept a middleman as part of the process and don't go directly to the distributor. If adults would allow their children to directly deal with a higher power, instead of forcing organized religion on them, there would be a greater faith among our population. If parents allowed their children to organically develop a relationship with a higher power, millions of children would avoid the emotional and physical abuse they receive from their relationships with the church.

Lesson learned: By deceiving ourselves on what a relationship really is, we are doing an insurmountable amount of short and long-term damage. Damage doesn't just occur when we want to extract ourselves from relationships, it affects us throughout the entire relationship. Misrepresenting a relationship causes pain and heartache. If we viewed relationships as transactions, we wouldn't resent people when they choose to take their business elsewhere. To look at what connects people and why it connects them allows us to go into every situation, circumstance, and relationship with our eyes and minds wide open. Jumping into a relationship, and then trying, without knowing how, to extract ourselves from it is the equivalent of jumping into the deep end of the pool, and then realizing we don't know how to swim. At that point, it's often too late and we end up drowning.

CHAPTER THIRTEEN

The Purpose of Communication

Communication has always been represented as the key to a relationship. Contrary to common belief, communication is the most over-rated and destructive aspect of a relationship. People don't communicate with each other, they just force their thoughts and opinions on another human being while despising someone doing the same to them. When people believe they're communicating with someone else, they're really using someone else as a conduit to communicate with themselves. Researchers theorize that the average person does not listen past the seventh word. If this is accurate, then how in good conscience can anyone say the key to a good relationship is communication? We're taught that communicating isn't enough: we need to communicate honestly. I couldn't disagree more. The times that people are most disappointed, angry, and frustrated with us coincide with the times that we are the most honest with them. The people who demand that we be honest are often the same ones who punish us when we are. Realizing people are going to be disappointed with us, whether we're honest or dishonest, leaves us in a personal quandary. Every time someone has caught me in a lie, they've expressed how disappointed they are that I didn't trust them enough to tell them the truth. From my perspective, it's not an issue of trust, it's their inability to accept the truth. We don't lie to people because we want to, we do it because we fear blow-back, knowing they are not emotionally and psychologically equipped to handle the truth. Beyond the lies that we tell other people is the lie that we tell ourselves: we've convinced ourselves that we lie to spare another person's feelings, but the truth is we lie to spare our own.

Example: One day a member of my gym wanted to talk. I spent more time conversing with my members than I did training them. She gave me a laundry list of all the issues she had with her husband. When she concluded, she asked for my opinion. Before I answered, I knew she either wanted me to validate her opinion or sympathize with her. I replied that she must have been a terrible judge of character to marry someone with so many faults. She became agitated, having assumed that my answer would coincide with her opinion of her husband. All I did was hold her accountable for what she told me. She gave me more than twenty reasons why she had a problem with her husband. I used those reasons to lay out my response. I told her that the average person may be fooled by someone who has three or four faults, but it's impossible to overlook the number of faults she alleged her husband had unless she chose to. I told her that it said a lot more about her character than it did her husband's. Like most people, she became upset when my answer reflected poorly on her. This, again, is why we lie to people. We rarely tell people what they need to hear because it only ends up getting turned back on us. Communication has become nothing more than avoiding conflict.

My interaction with this member is a prime example of how communication is overrated. First, she came into my office with a predetermined agenda. Second, she asked me to listen and give her my honest feedback, when that's the last thing she wanted. Third, I listened to the entire conversation, never interrupting, so I could give her an unbiased answer. Fourth, when I gave her my unbiased answer, it immediately created conflict. She became angry at me for doing exactly what she asked me to do, which was listen and give her honest feedback. The reason I listened without interrupting was, so I could use her words as evidence instead of just rendering an opinion. It is impossible to verbally communicate with people. You're punished when you lie, and you're severely punished when you tell the truth.

Lessons learned: When people ask us for information, they're really asking for affirmation and validation. The truth is the first thing that people ask for, but the last thing they want to hear. Every person is born with a survival instinct, and it goes against human nature to harm ourselves, which often occurs when we tell someone the truth.

THE TRUTH IS A LIE

CHAPTER FOURTEEN

The Most Dishonest Form of Communication

S tudies show that non-verbal communication is the truest form of communication. The problem with non-verbal communication is that it requires people to be patient and attentive, which are two qualities that most people lack. We are a society that solely relies on verbal communication, which is the most dishonest form of communication. We talk but we don't listen; we listen, but we rarely hear; we rarely hear, and never see. Verbal communication should be like a GPS system. It should be direct, concise, and get us from point A to point B in an efficient and timely manner. Society makes this impossible. When we are direct with people, they are likely to respond by verbalizing their displeasure, making what should be a simple conversation difficult, then they become heavy-handed doling out their frustrations on us. Therefore, we lie as a self-defense mechanism, prioritizing self-survival over conveying the truth to others.

People who demand us to be honest: parents, teachers, and authority figures are the same ones who condition us to lie and punish us when we tell the truth. People who demand we tell them the truth are oblivious to the fact that they are the reason we lie, which is the irony of the situation. The punishments I received for being honest far out-weighed any punishment I received for telling a lie. We quickly learn that lying often accomplishes two things: attaining what we want from someone while avoiding repercussions. Lying isn't enough. We need to soften the lie with language that makes it more palatable for the person hearing it.

Example #1: When I asked for something from my parents, they would always say "Don't beat around the bush, if you want something, just be direct and ask us." The problem with that statement is that every time I directly asked for something, I didn't receive it. My parents viewed me as being indirect and indecisive with my language, never factoring in that my history with them created this form of communication. Not only did I have to lie to my parents to get what I wanted and avoid punish-ment, but I had to do it in the most indirect, meandering way. I always felt like a racecar driver around my parents, having to shift gears and weave in-and-out of traffic to reach my destination.

Example #2: My dad owned a restaurant and worked for 16 plus hours a day, which made my mother responsible for my upbringing. My relationship with my dad was strained, and my relationship with my mother was functional, but not healthy. During one encounter, I realized how unhealthy the relationship was.

I was punished by my dad, and he sent me to my room, telling me: no dinner, no television, no playing with your toys, sit on the end of your bed and contemplate what you've done, and most importantly, don't leave your room. In the corner of my room, I had a bookcase. Be-hind the bookcase there was ample crawl space that I could easily get in and out of, making it impossible to find me if I chose to hide there. After a while, I heard my dad walking towards my room. Like any kid, you learn the sound of your parent's walk and you quickly learn to differentiate between the two. Before my dad reached my door, I crawled behind the bookcase. I could sense my dad looking around the room and heard him cursing under his breath. After he left my room, he started screaming for my mother, yelling that I wasn't anywhere to be found. I heard my mother's voice getting louder, telling my dad that was impossible, she had just looked in on me, omitting the fact that she had snuck in food for me. My dad yelled back, "Well, he's not here now," and I heard them both scurrying to my room. By this time, I had crawled out from behind the bookcase and was sitting on my bed. My mother immediately said to my dad, "I told you he was here," which agitated him even more. He then yelled at my mother, "I can see that, but he wasn't here before." He then looked at me and said, "Where did you go?" to which I replied, "I've been here the whole time." My dad's question was ambiguous enough to allow me to tell the truth even though I knew what he was really asking. He looked at my mother with disgust and left the room. My mother sat down next to me and asked, "Where did you go?" My gut and her aggressive body language told me to not trust her. My mother instinctively felt my apprehension, causing her to say, "It's ok, you can trust me. Tell me where you went." I got up, walked my mother to the bookcase, and showed her the crawl space. She said, "Why do you do this to your dad?" to which I replied, "No matter what I do, I'm going to be in trouble, so I might as well get something out of it." My mother walked to my door, and before leaving, turned to me and said, "Don't worry, I'll take care of it." Boy did she! Before she even made it to the hallway, she was yelling for my dad. My initial instinct was that my mom was going to throw me under the bus, but I didn't realize she was going to back over me three or four times. My dad walked into my room and my mother walked him right over to the crawl space.

That was the last day I was ever direct and honest with my mother. I viewed my mother as the buffer between my dad and myself. That buffer had now been removed. What hurt me wasn't that my mother betrayed my confidence, it's that she did it within seconds of telling me I could trust her. It would've been one thing for her to succumb to my dad verbally berating her, but she initiated the betrayal. At that moment, my mother went from being a soft-landing spot to a mark, someone that I now viewed through the prism of what I could attain from her. I can't recall one conversation with my mother after that encounter that wasn't disingenuous. There's a cliché that states, "You can shear a sheep many times, only skin it once." I felt my mother had skinned me.

In hindsight, I could've been more tolerant and forgiving of my mother. Not condoning what she did, but not using her betrayal as an excuse to punish her for my issues with my dad. This experience taught me how detrimental honest verbal communication can be.

The first lesson learned: Adults demand that we be honest and then use that honesty to punish us. Looking back, my instincts regarding my mother were correct. I didn't fear reprisal from my dad, I feared betrayal by my mother, and I realized I opened that door by trusting her and being honest.

The second lesson learned: These experiences we have with our parents, and adults, are something we encounter the rest of our lives. We learn that directness and honesty are asked for, but never valued. At the same time, we realize that dishonesty and indirectness are verbally frowned upon, but often directly and indirectly rewarded.

CHAPTER FIFTEEN

Positions of Power

C hildren are in a completely inferior position. They are never on an equal playing field with adults. Both parties understand this. Adults don't view children as equals, they view them as subordinates. Adults' superiority over children is both physical and psychological. My father was never physical with me, but he would constantly raise his voice and invade my physical space for the sole purpose of intimidating me. It was like a mere mortal living in Jurassic Park. Whenever there was a disagreement, my father would end it by invading my space, knowing that I would submit. When children are dominated and forced to relent, it adds to the insecurity and inferiority complex that many of them already have. Bullies often target a weak and inferior opponent, intimidating them into submission. When you're on the wrong end of the bullying, you're not concerned with understanding the bully's mindset.

Example: As stated before, my dad owned a restaurant dealing with the public sixteen hours a day. After a sixteen-hour day, the last thing my dad wanted to do was deal with me. The initial mistake my dad made wasn't an unwillingness to change his behavior, it's that he had more children than he should have. The second mistake my dad made was not changing his behavior once he had kids. Having children requires adults to completely modify their behavior, schedule, and lifestyle. The realities of life make this virtually impossible. Many adults want to continue living the life they've always lived after having children. This is a decision that should be made before having children but often isn't. The child is the one who suffers from this lack of foresight.

At night, my dad's only concern was decompressing and re-energizing for the following day. This left little to no time for parenting. Early on I was told not to bother and interrupt my dad, and that if he wanted to speak with me, he would initiate the conversation. Being in a position of power, my dad dictated all exchanges. Not understanding how difficult his life and profession were, I was left to assume that I was the problem. I would have understood the situation had my dad taken the time to have a simple conversation with me. What people in a position of power fail to realize is that the people they are interacting with don't ask for much. The simplest gesture can achieve monumental results. Instead, many people in a position of power wield that power like a sword, slashing everything in its path.

Lesson learned: My dad's abuse of his position of power caused me to look at him like any other person. The illusion that many children have of their parents was shattered, allowing me to look at him from a realistic and logical perspective. These encounters accelerated my psychological growth while stunting my emotional maturity. As an adult, I am now a study in duality. Logically, I'm often advanced beyond my years, while emotionally, in many aspects, I've never grown. My upbringing created this division, but it's solely my responsibility to fix.

CHAPTER SIXTEEN

The Family Dynamic

Many families have multiple children. When confronted, parents say they love each child equally. This fallacy is psychologically unacceptable, and personally and emotionally impossible. In our family, it was as clear as glass. My dad's affinity and affection for my oldest sister was impossible not to see. What pained me as a child wasn't the way my dad treated my oldest sister, it was that I had the capability to compare it with how he treated me. My dad's behavior was consistent in how he treated the two of us, but the two treatments were completely different. This left me, as the youngest child, believing the problem was me. The normal family dynamic is the baby of the family is usually the spoiled, pampered one. In my family, every positive emotion that my dad conveyed went to my oldest sister.

Example: Teachers will often say they don't pick favorites, they treat every student the same, and their opinion of the students isn't based on the students' behavior acquiescing to theirs. This is often not the case. Teachers favor the student who does what they say, falls in line, and modifies their behavior to the expectations of the teacher. The cliché 'teacher's pet' came from somewhere. This also occurs in the home. Parents gravitate towards the child who thinks like them, acts like them, does things in a fashion that's acceptable to them, and makes their life easier. I was none of these. What I will never know is if I was born defiant and obstinate, or if I incorporated those qualities based on the affection that I never received. I often ask myself, "Are we a product of our environment or is our environment a product of us?" I realize now that answer is different for everyone based on how they were raised and if they were controlled.

Lesson learned: This internalization taught me that it's impossible to look at two people and feel the same level of emotion, even if they are your children or family members. The painful realization is that I couldn't understand this at an early age. I viewed my dad's dismissiveness towards me as something that I had earned or deserved. I couldn't process my dad's lack of affection towards me until it was too late. My dad's elevated affection towards my sister was something that every human being encounters and experiences but something a child should never encounter.

CHAPTER SEVENTEEN

Youth is Wasted on the Young

How often do adults try to relate to the younger generation? The answer is: hardly ever. The emphasis is always put on the child to understand the adult. Children are not psychologically or emotionally equipped to understand themselves, let alone the thought process of an adult. Why is the onus put on the child to understand the adult? The answer is simple: an adult does not want to take the time it requires to understand where a child is coming from and who they are trying to become.

Another underlying theme in this book is time. Many people don't value time, but some do. Forcing a child to conform to the adult minimizes the investment of time that the adult must make while robbing the child of the ability to spread their wings. This robs the child of their youth and innocence and has lifelong ramifications.

Example: Once while cleaning the garage with my dad, I asked him what his biggest regret was. He replied, "Leaving the Navy." Not needing any prompting, he expounded on how much he loved the Navy, how he loved traveling the world, and the freedom and independence it provided him. By this acknowledgment, he was stating that he regretted getting married and having a family because those things occurred after leaving the service.

My dad was the youngest of two boys. His mother idolized his older brother, my Uncle Tommy, the way my dad idolized my oldest sister. The Navy provided him a sense of self-worth and pride that his mother had taken from him, the same way I felt he had taken mine from me. This lack of self-worth made my dad feel that he wasn't worthy of the dreams that he aspired to. Instead of staying in the Navy, he met and married my mother and chose to work in her father's business. Even after obtaining ownership of the restaurant from my grandfather, I know my dad felt unfulfilled. My dad was extremely successful but was living a life mapped out by others, all driven by the lack of affection and attention he received in his youth. He went from conforming to his mother, to conforming to my grandfather, to conforming to my mother. My dad's youth wasn't just taken from him, he was made to feel fortunate with any opportunity that presented itself. This led to a lifetime of choices shaped by others.

On multiple occasions, I felt that my dad's discomfort, agitation, restlessness, and overall disposition was based on choosing the wrong life path. If he had received the proper affection in his childhood and not had been suppressed in his formative years, the course of his life may have gone in a completely different direction. Many in society face this dilemma daily.

Lesson learned: In the Wizard of Oz, Dorothy's yellow brick road was chosen for her. Dorothy mistakenly believed it would lead to her lifelong destination. In life, our road isn't paved in gold, is often chosen by someone else, and rarely leads to self-fulfillment.

CHAPTER EIGHTEEN

Behavior Modification

Parents often present a utopian world to their children, feeling they're protecting them from the world that really exists, when selfishly, they're prioritizing the time required to explain the world as it really is. It requires no energy to explain this misrepresented viewpoint. Shielding anyone from the realities of life can cause an insurmountable amount of damage. This protection is illogical, but aligns with human nature because at their core, people are lazy.

Example: I've watched several documentaries on the serial killer Ted Bundy. For those who may not remember, the movie *The Silence of the Lambs* was a loose semi-biographical film of Bundy's life, killing spree, and his work with FBI profilers pertaining to cases of other serial killers. Bundy approached many of his female victims wearing a self-made cast on one of his arms, giving him the appearance of being physically impaired. He would ask his victims to help him move his boat, portraying that he was incapable of doing it himself. His victims agreed to help him at the cost of their lives, except for one woman, who was fortunate to escape. I can only imagine the confliction these women felt when he approached them. Instinctively, they had to be concerned with their safety. I'm assuming these instincts came in direct conflict with the upbringing and behavior modification that these young women received. These abductions and murders could have been avoided if these women had been told at an early age that people aren't always trustworthy, often have ulterior motives, and, in some instances, are looking to harm them. Instead of being told that people are good, kind, and compassionate, we should be taught to protect ourselves at all costs. We should be told that helping other people is a noble gesture but can be harmful to us, hence the cliché "No good deed goes unpunished." If these women had been taught to see the world for what it really was, they might be alive today. Instead, these women were probably concerned with how they would be perceived if they refused to help, therefore they risked their lives prioritizing perception over preservation.

Bundy was extremely intelligent and manipulative, aware of societal norms and perceptions, and used those to his benefit. He would approach women in the middle of summer on a populated beach in full view of hundreds of people. Not one woman followed him unwillingly to their demise. The inner conflict they must have felt succumbed to the illogical behavior modification they had received. Eliminate the modification, and you eliminate life-threatening situations. The one victim who escaped Bundy's grasp wasn't approached on a beach, she was approached in a vacant parking lot. He represented himself as a law enforcement officer, telling her that she needed to go to the police station with him to make a statement. He told her that someone had tried to break into her vehicle and showed her a badge when she requested identification. He was dressed in plain clothes and was driving his now infamous yellow VW Bug. She testified later to police that his badge looked fake, his attire caused her great concern, and that she didn't believe his story that he was driving an undercover vehicle. Even after all these red flags, she chose to override her instincts, fortunately, not to her demise.

Lesson learned: Our instincts and our behavior modification are in constant conflict. Our gut is our instinct, our head is our modification. If you eliminate the head, you are left with the gut. You eliminate modification, you eliminate conflict. The smallest deviation from our instincts can lead to the most catastrophic results. The lack of honesty that occurs in our upbringing often has adverse consequences in our adulthood. The ripple-in-the-pond theory pertains to every one of our lives. The initial ripple, if it's caused by lies and misrepresentation, leads to each subsequent ripple, expanding that initial lie or misrepresentation. When things occur, we often compartmentalize and look at each individual occurrence without asking ourselves, "Why did this occur?" and, more importantly, "What was the point of origin?" Everything that we do, including our behavior and mistakes, can be traced back to our earliest teachings. Childhood modification is difficult to overcome. The best thing we can do is immediately rip out the hard-wiring of what we have been taught and replace it with the wiring of our instincts and life experiences. When we do that, we have a greater opportunity to remove ourselves from harm's way.

CHAPTER NINETEEN

The Dangers of Conformity

Control, leverage, and power are keywords in society. People wield these like a sword, with the goal being conformity. People don't choose to conform, it's often forced upon them, with punishment and reprisal occurring the minute someone shows an ounce of individuality. This punishment causes us, through conditioning, to conform before we are even asked or forced to.

People in a position of power want to maintain that position. The best way to accomplish this task is the suppression of others. The goal of many adults is to condition children, so they no longer must work to get them to conform; the child simply, through conditioning, falls in line. Conformity doesn't occur after the child starts asking questions, it occurs before questioning can begin, averting an uprising before it begins. Power is rarely handled responsibly. The more power that someone has, the more likely they are to abuse it. No one has more power over a child than an adult. It's equivalent to the power that a warden has over a prisoner. Prisoners' lives revolve around someone else's schedule, as do children's. The only time that people in society don't ask you to conform is when your lack of conformity benefits them. If people feel that they can benefit emotionally, personally, or financially from your lack of conformity, then your lack of conformity will be accepted, even if you are not.

Example: I love the classic tales that Disney and other companies produced. One of my favorites is *Rudolph, the Red-Nosed Reindeer*. I like watching these classics on my own because I like to psychoanalyze them and extract my own messages from them, not the message that the creators and others want us to incorporate. Rudolph is the perfect example of conformity and how someone different, is mocked, ridiculed, and shunned to the point of complete isolation. Rudolph like many people in society, tried to change and mask who he was to fit in. He did this solely to avoid the bullying that was occurring. When he tried to mask and hide who he was, it didn't ingratiate him to the other reindeer, it merely alleviated, to a degree, the abuse that he had to endure. Only when the weather turned catastrophic to the point where Rudolph's abnormality became a necessity was, he finally needed. Rudolph was never accepted, he was simply tolerated because there were no other viable options.

The underlying message of this classic is what occurs to many in society. People change their behavior, demeanor, thought process, and appearance to avoid being persecuted. Our concern shouldn't be other people's comfort with us, it should be our comfort with ourselves. Rudolph's abnormality was a threat to everyone else because of their insecurities but ended up being taken out on him, which is also common. Without the benefits that Rudolph provided, and the circumstances that created the need for his uniqueness, the treatment towards him would never have changed; in fact, it probably would have worsened. Society wants us to conform for two reasons. One, it makes their lives easier. Two, because people are insecure, and individuality is threatening.

Lesson learned: People's insecurities and issues should never cause us to conform. Insecurities can never be eased by someone else.

Rudolph's uniqueness was taken advantage of because the situation ne-
cessitated it. That type of situation often occurs in the movies, but rarely
occurs in real life. In life, people rarely want to understand uniqueness,
they just want to suppress and ridicule it, driving many people into a
state of depression, instead of rejoicing in their individuality. We can't
wait, like in the movies, for the opportunity to present itself for our
uniqueness to come to the forefront. We need to find comfort in embracing our individuality even when society does not.

CHAPTER TWENTY

Religion is Above Reproach

R he laws of religion look just like the laws of society. They were created to keep people in check and to deny, to a large degree, individual thought. Religion's true hold over society is that it holds the ultimate trump card – eternal salvation or eternal damnation. We've spent a lot of time discussing control, but we've spent no time on guilt. Guilt is a psychological tool that people use when trying to control another. Everyone has a story where they were controlled by guilt. Where do you think the term 'peer pressure' came from? The church often uses guilt to emotionally, psychologically, and financially control their parishioners. In school, we advance to a higher grade each year with the goal of graduating and tackling life on our own. With the church, there is no advancement, no climbing to the next rung, no graduating or tackling religion on your own. If the church advances a parishioner's relationship with God, that parishioner would graduate and no longer need the church. And if the parishioner no longer needed the church, the church would no longer exist.

War, public scandals, and societal crises have all occurred under the guise of religion, and the church is aware of the stranglehold they have on society. They have taken advantage of their position to the detriment of the people they have been entrusted to help. The reason the church and religion can take advantage of their parishioners is that their parishioners are not just loyal to the church, they're blindly loyal. Look at the illegalities that have occurred pertaining to the Catholic Church, their priests, and the abuse of minors. This abuse may have been perpetrated by priests in positions of power, but the responsibility equally falls in the lap of the adults who allowed the abuse to occur.

When I was eight or nine, I wanted to go camping with one of my friends who lived down the street. His brother was going to be our chaperone. My parents didn't allow me to go, saying they didn't know my friend's brother well enough. Every time my parents took a position it perplexed me, always contradicting a previous position they had taken. My parents had a problem with my friend's brother, who they hardly knew, but they never had a problem suggesting church retreats with adults they never met. When I would tell my parents, "You know his older brother a lot better than you know our pastor," their automatic response was, "Harry, he's a priest." That was the beginning and the end of the discussion. These are the same people who told me to never talk to strangers and to never trust someone I didn't know. What they should have told me is, "Never talk to strangers or go anywhere with someone you don't know unless they're wearing a collar." The reason abuse was, and is, so prevalent in the Catholic Church is there were many people like my parents, who prioritized religion over logic.

One of the biggest mistakes we make is attributing characteristics to people based on the position they hold in society and the apparel that comes with that position. People often abuse positions of power based on society's unconditional trust and respect for those positions. Politicians, doctors, lawyers, teachers, and people in the clergy all fall under this umbrella. Every job in society should follow a series of checks and balances, especially the jobs where public trust is involved. These positions have two things in common: they aren't subjected to checks and balances, and they often go unsupervised.

When I went to church, the visual layout was the first thing I noticed. Freud said, "There are no coincidences," and I agree. In the orthodox church, the pastor stands behind his pulpit, which is elevated to such a height that it not only allows him to look down on his parishioners but more importantly, it forces the parishioners to look up to him. This isn't an accident. Another strategy that the church incorporates is expecting their parishioners to kneel. This creates a god-like experience, rendering the parishioners helpless.

Example: I have seen the movie "Spotlight" several times. *Spotlight* was a division of the Boston Globe that focused on major stories in the Boston area. In the movie, Spotlight focused on the Catholic Church and their abuse of children over decades. As the movie evolved, the focus shifted from the abuse to the insurmountable amount of money and man-hours the Church invested in the cover-up of these abuses. The cover-up didn't stop with the priests and the Archdiocese, it went all the way to the Vatican. The Archdiocese developed relationships with the police, government officials, and the local newspapers so that when abuses occurred, they could leverage those relationships to keep the abuse under wraps. The more Spotlight uncovered, the greater the pressure the Archdiocese exerted to suppress the story. The abuse of power occurred because religious figures in this country are considered above reproach, which allows them to abuse their power while accumulating unbelievable wealth.

Lesson learned: The higher someone's status is in the community or in society, the more liberties and abuses occur. There is no higher status in the community, society, or the planet than that of religion, and no one is more aware of this than the church. There is no condoning the people in a position of power abusing that power, but society is partially responsible for blindly trusting these people.

I love Spiderman. From the comic book to the cartoon series to the movies, the one phrase that's conveyed to Peter Parker by his Uncle Ben is, "With great power, comes great responsibility." People in positions of power have the choice of wielding the sword for the greater good of society instead of themselves. We can't control someone abusing power once they're in that position, but we can control whether we blindly worship those people. When we worship someone based on the uniform they wear or the position they hold, we can't be upset when they abuse that position and us.

CHAPTER TWENTY-ONE

Human Nature

I love mob movies, and my favorite is *The Godfather*. The first time I saw it, I watched it with my mother. After the movie, all my mother wanted to talk about was the performances, and all I wanted to talk about was the message. The message in mob movies is equivalent to the message of human nature. It begins with love, loyalty, friendship, and honor. It ends with betrayal, murder, manipulation, and everyone ratting each other out to save their own behind. Every mob movie has a hierarchy, from the lowest foot soldier to the head of the family. This hierarchy exists in society as well. The higher you are on the ladder, the more entrenched you become in protecting that position.

All the President's Men is another of my favorite movies. The movie is told from the perspective of two Washington Post reporters, Bob Woodward and Carl Bernstein, who were assigned to investigate the Watergate break-in. As the story unfolds, the cover-up eventually leads the reporters to President Richard Nixon. To me, the most intriguing part of the movie is how many people lied, manipulated, and were coerced at the behest of President Nixon and his advisors. This included every law enforcement agency whose duty was to uphold the law, but who broke it at nearly every turn. Nixon's top two advisers, Bob Haldeman and John

Ehrlichman, were blindly loyal to him, which didn't stop Nixon from throwing them to the wolves when the investigation led to his doorstep. This is identical to almost every situation we observe and encounter growing up, whether it's our parents, teachers, or anyone in a position of power. I noticed that when people in a position of power did something wrong and repercussions were lying on their doorstep, they immediately looked for someone in an inferior position to be their scapegoat. The Watergate break-in was the incident where five individuals were hired by the Republican National Committee (RNC) to break into the Watergate building with the purpose of installing wiretapping equipment to record conversations of the Democratic National Committee (DNC). When the break-in occurred, no one knew the full extent of what would be uncovered. Woodward and Bernstein eventually realized that the break-in was one event in a series of illegalities by the RNC that began eighteen months earlier. When people are caught doing something that's improper or illegal, whether it be cheating, drinking and driving, stealing, or anything else that society would deem as wrong, it's rarely the first time those events have occurred; it's just the first time they've been caught. A perfect example of this in society is law enforcement. The job description for law enforcement officers is to protect and serve the public. If this were true, then the relationship between law enforcement officers and society wouldn't be as toxic. The relationship should be seamless: they get paid to protect us, and we need protection. This relationship is anything but seamless because human nature was never factored into the equation.

Example #1: In the chapter on religion, I stated that we should not judge the uniform, but the person wearing it. Police officers are in a position of power, and they have often abused that power because we, as a society, have allowed it. We have chosen to look at the badge and uniform, and not the person and their behavior. An unhealthy environment has been created because of the life-threatening positions that people encounter with law enforcement. The difference between law enforcement and the church is that society has the choice to not attend church. Society does not have the choice to avoid law enforcement, empowering them even more. Once we are confronted by law enforcement, we often submit, prioritizing our personal safety over their abuse of power, which the job and uniform have granted them. If human nature is to do what is in one's best interest, then people in positions of power, especially those who go unsupervised, will almost always abuse that power.

Example #2: As stated, my dad owned a restaurant and, although we were never close, I had immense respect for how hard he worked and how disciplined he was: two qualities that I lacked in spades. Every Sunday, I would go to the restaurant with him and my job was to clean it from top to bottom, even if it took me the entire day. Within two hours of arriving, my dad would always head towards the back of the restaurant, telling me to stay up front while he talked with two men who entered through the rear. One Sunday, I crept back and saw that the two gentlemen my dad was talking to were plain clothed policemen. I found it suspicious that they were not in uniform, and Sunday was the day the restaurant was closed to the public. I witnessed my dad handing the officers a large box filled with cigarettes, liquor, food, and other assorted items. I also witnessed my dad handing one of the officers an envelope. As they left, my dad turned around and caught me eavesdropping. After they were gone, my dad sat me down and said this was what was required to run his business. I was thirteen or fourteen when this occurred. My first thought wasn't that my dad was paying off police officers, it was that my dad took the opportunity to teach me a life lesson on human nature instead of punishing me for disobeying his order. After my dad explained what had occurred, I asked him why he simply didn't turn the officers in. He responded with two words: "Human nature." He said, "If I do that, it will be a lose-lose for me. If I turn them in, their superiors are going to protect their own, and it will be devastating to my business." I asked, "How could it be devastating to your business?" He replied,

"Because those same officers will walk in one day with the Health Department and shut me down for a week or two simply for informing someone of their illegal activities."

One of my dad's best friends, Fred Shane, was a long-time police officer with the Akron Police Department. When I asked him why he was such good friends with a policeman, after all he had experienced, he replied, "In over 20 years of being in business, Mr. Shane is one of two officers who didn't extort me. In fact, Mr. Shane wouldn't even take a free meal." After I was finished working on Sundays, my dad would make me breakfast, and he was an A-level chef. Mr. Shane would often come in and have breakfast with us, Sunday often being his day off as well. Never once did he not pay for the meal, despite my dad's resistance to taking money from his friend.

Lessons learned: Mr. Shane was an honorable and ethical man, not just an honorable and ethical police officer. His morality was admirable, but it could not overcome the lack of morality that I saw from the police officers and the extortion that my dad dealt with on a weekly basis. Mr. Shane should have been the norm, not the exception, but when you factor in human nature, Mr. Shane becomes the exception, not the norm. Human nature is easily predictable. In the book *The Art of War*, Sun Tzu states, "Every battle is won before it's fought." When you apply this to human beings and human nature, you can often predict people's behavior before it occurs.

CHAPTER TWENTY–TWO

Beliefs and Opinions

The minute someone states something as fact, I know it's their opinion. We have become a society that believes our opinions are not just right for us, they are right for everyone. The arrogance of believing that our every thought is a fact is one of our biggest character flaws. People expound on a myriad of subjects as if they're experts. The truth is there is very little if any, research done on the topics that we pontificate on daily. If we do not learn anything new past the age of seven, then how can we be experts on everything? What we profess are facts are nothing more than regurgitated thoughts, beliefs, and opinions that have been passed down from one generation to the next. The only fact we can assert is that there are few facts in our opinions. Opinions are often based on the insecurity of the person giving them. Our beliefs and perceptions are tied to a self–serving narrative which is tied to a self–serving agenda. All it takes to have opinions accepted as fact is to be the first to say them, to repeat them over an extended period, or to develop a large following and have them convey your beliefs on your be-half.

Example #1: From the beginning of time, racism has existed. It began with mankind and has been reinforced by the dictionary. Noah

Webster, the creator of Webster's Dictionary, was white. His dictionary's definitions of *black* and *white* are filled with racial overtones. His definition of *black* is 'characterized by the absence of light and thoroughly sinister or evil.' In direct contrast, his definition of *white* is 'free from spot or blemish; free of color, and light or pallid in color.' We've been told that if something is in print, it must be true. Many of the things we see in print are nothing more than the opinions of the person who wrote them, the dictionary being no exception. Legally one must trademark and copyright a word, name, or a phrase to own it. Webster copyrighted and trademarked his words, phrases, and definitions by putting them in print. Webster is not the only culprit to render beliefs for his own benefit.

Example #2: Adolf Hitler is one of the most vilified individuals the world has ever known. Hitler was the patriarch of Germany and the diabolical mastermind of the Aryan Race, who was responsible for the Nazi party and the mass murder of Jewish people. There is no denying who Hitler was, what he did, and how horrific he and his crimes were. In America, we vilify him, as we should, but in contrast, we celebrate and idolize Christopher Columbus. Columbus's discovery of America led to the death of "somewhere between 60,000,000 and 80,000,000 natives [American] ...were dead," (Jennings, 1994). Although Columbus's true intent is still widely debated, the result was, like Hitler's, the near extinction of an entire race. The common belief is to view Columbus as a pioneer and hero, solely based on the personal benefit attained by his discovery. That benefit is so profound that we have turned it into a national holiday. Native Americans and people who live outside of the United States have different opinions regarding Columbus.

Our beliefs are rooted in self-benefit and perception, not fact. This ties to the Sherlock Holmes Theory in reverse that was discussed in chapter four. Once a person conveys a belief, no evidence to the contrary will shake their foundation. People's concern isn't about being right, it's about never being proven wrong. Like a tick or leech, people will dig in

THE TRUTH IS A LIE

once they've developed their belief system.

The lesson learned is that we have never learned our lesson. We are more close-minded, defensive, and opinionated than we have ever been. We do not seek information, we seek validation. We no longer want to discuss, we just want other people to sign off on everything we think and feel. Beliefs and opinions should rarely be conveyed. We should instead focus on facts and evidence. But those require time, research, and depth of thought, which is why we convey opinions and beliefs instead.

CHAPTER TWENTY-THREE

Internal and External Conflicts

Psychologists say that when people acquiesce to someone else's needs and demands, it's often to avoid conflict. I believe psychologists are partially correct. When we acquiesce to someone's demands, we are avoiding short-term conflict, but the seeds of conflict that have already been planted will have negative long-term ramifications. As our internal conflict grows, so does the behavior of the person we have conditioned by avoiding the initial confrontation. Conflict isn't created by someone imposing their will on us, it is created when we allow and accept that imposition. As adults, the responsibility is on us for allowing someone to impose their will on us. As children, the responsibility always falls on the shoulders of the person imposing the will. We allow this imposition because we were punished as children for standing up to it. This pattern has become ingrained in us to the point that it takes an unbelievable amount of effort and resolve to reverse the trend. Conflict is unavoidable, it can only be delayed, and delaying it often creates a larger dilemma. Once conflict occurs, the more dominant party, physically and financially, almost always prevails.

Human behavior is like the foundation of a house. If that foundation is flawed and you continue to build upon it, the flaw will only expand in size, and the flawed foundation will eventually weaken and crumble. A flawed foundation cannot be repaired, it must be demolished and then completely rebuilt. Suppression creates a crack in our foundation. Every day that we allow suppression is another brick on top of our flawed foundation. It's impossible for us, as children, to stop this suppression, and the people who are putting bricks on our flawed foundation are aware of this.

Example: In my teens, I played on a baseball team coached and managed by my friend's father. I started and played first base. Infrequently, my mother would attend a game. During one of these games, we were dominating the other team. My teammates and I were all playing well. Because the score was so lopsided, our manager decided to give the reserves an opportunity to play. The minute my mother realized I wasn't in the game, she began complaining. Her behavior was embarrassing to me and impossible for anyone to ignore. Not wanting the situation to escalate, the manager looked at me as if to say, "Harry, fix this problem." Knowing that confronting my mother would only inflame the situation, I walked out of the dugout, sat beside her, and begged her to stop. I explained that the manager took everyone out, it was not just me, and that the reserves hardly ever get an opportunity to play. I told her that her behavior was embarrassing for everyone on my team. I felt at the time that I did the best I could. My mother disregarded my opinion, her only concern was to express what she wanted to say, the way she wanted to say it. Trying to stifle that only made my situation worse. After returning to the dugout, my mother's anger shifted from the manager to me.

On the drive home, my mother used every second to admonish me for confronting and embarrassing her. I immediately tuned my mother out and spent the entire trip debating the benefits and consequences of having confronted her. I didn't realize the life-long ramifications that her behavior and my confrontation caused until later. Arriving home, my mother voiced her complete displeasure about my behavior to my dad, omitting everything that she had done, prompting my dad to turn his ire towards me.

These two admonishments were only the beginning. The following year I was cut from the same team I previously started for. The day I was cut, my mother asked me how practice was. I told her I had been cut from the team. My mother thought I was joking since it was the first day of practice. She replied, "How do you go from being a starter to being cut on the first day?" Incensed and frustrated, I pointed my finger towards her and said, "You're the reason." My mother knew exactly what I meant. Not wanting to take responsibility, just like the previous year, my mother simply walked away. No longer fearing immediate conflict, I followed her, stating that the headache she caused the manager the previous year had resulted in my being cut from the team.

Years later, my assumption was proven correct. During a dinner at my friend's house, his father apologized for cutting me from the team and punishing me for my mother's behavior. I respected his honesty, but it did nothing to diminish my anger and pain. Years earlier, I knew confronting my mother would not suppress her behavior. Years later, I realized that my friend's father's failure to confront my mother and punishment of me was just as reprehensible. Many people avoid confrontation and conflict because it does not resolve the issue and often makes their situation worse. The problem the manager had was not with my confrontation, it was with my mother's behavior. I never played competitive baseball again. It is a decision that I regret to this day. I am embarrassed that I chose to avoid outer conflict at the expense of a lifetime of inner conflict. I am accountable for my actions and I am embarrassed that I was so weak that I gave up on something I loved to avoid future confrontations with my parents.

Lesson learned: We avoid conflict for many reasons: weakness, fear, anxiety, repercussions, insecurity, and the seeking of approval, but the foundation of avoiding conflict is often suppression and reprisal. Multiple sources convey that we are born with only two fears. That means that every other fear that we have has been ingrained in us. Every person prioritizes their fears differently, and on the top of my priority scale was the fear of reprisal. That fear was based on the short and long-term ramifications I would suffer by confronting the person who had created the reason for my confrontation. This ripple-in-the-pond effect never turns out in our favor. Avoiding short-term conflict and confrontation may lessen the immediate reprisal but will often cause long-term inner conflict. Inner conflict is often created by avoiding the people who should be our source of comfort.

CHAPTER TWENTY-FOUR

Inconsistency in Humans

People are extremely consistent. The problem with society is that it does not view inconsistent behavior as consistent. Once you see someone's inconsistencies, that's who they truly are. Once you see who they truly are, you can consistently rely on those inconsistencies.

Example #1: What people say rarely matches what they do. Society views this as inconsistent, but logic will tell you that every time someone says something, it is almost guaranteed that they will do the opposite. The adage says, "Fool me once, shame on you, fool me twice, shame on me." Once we become aware of someone's patterns, no matter how inconsistent society may consider them, we can no longer punish them for refusing to change.

Example #2: If an employee is out one day per week, you can call them inconsistent. But the truth is, they consistently show up four times a week, which now puts the onus on the employer to determine the value of that employee. We refuse to see people's behavior for what it is because if we do, it puts the responsibility on us to decide their value in our life.

When we are listening and observing, all we hear and see is someone's inconsistencies, instead of recognizing that they are showing us who they are. Once we see someone's behavior, it forces us to make one of two choices: either accept it or remove ourselves from the equation. Most people choose a third option, which is to continue to blame and punish the person for being who they are. When you choose option C, what you are doing is punishing someone for not being who you want them to be. It is not someone's responsibility to behave in a way that makes us comfortable or to act in a way that we consider consistent, the onus and responsibility are on us to determine if we accept their behavior.

Example #3: The airlines. After 9/11, everyone complained about the lack of security at our airports, stating that was the reason terrorists were able to get on American airplanes. These are the same people now complaining that their rights are violated every time they go to the airport. This is the inconsistent consistent behavior that applies to every human being. People say one thing and do another: people want something until they get it; people complain but do nothing about it; people hate their lives, but never change anything; people critique everyone else, but never judge themselves. Our inability to view situations and people for what and who they are allows us to dispense blame, but never resolves the situation.

Example #4: Politicians and public figures. We are always demanding that politicians and public figures tell us the truth. History shows how disingenuous our demands are. Example: John F. Kennedy, Martin Luther King, Jr., and Malcolm X all paid the ultimate price for giving us what we asked for: the truth. These men stood up for what they believed in and gave society a glimpse of who they really were. The minute their beliefs and opinions clashed with those of society's, their days on this earth were numbered.

Lesson learned: When we view someone's behavior as inconsistent, it's because their behavior isn't what we want and often demand. That doesn't mean their behavior is inconsistent, it means our expectations are unrealistic. The mistake isn't with people's behavior, it's with our unwillingness to accept it.

CHAPTER TWENTY-FIVE

Perceptions

People say, "perception is reality". Perception may be our reality, but it is often the furthest thing from the truth. Perception is not how we see something, it is how we choose to see it. We are all subjective beings, which makes our perceptions and conclusions subjective. When we perceive something as a statement of fact, it rarely is, it is just *our* statement of fact.

The Sherlock Holmes Theory in reverse is based on people creating their own narrative and twisting the facts to fit that narrative. That it is exactly what we do with our perceptions. We choose to see something, then any fact that contradicts our perception is dismissed or contorted to align with what we want to see. The harder we try to convince ourselves that something is the truth, the more we know our words and thoughts are based on perception. These perceptions are created to mask our flaws and insecurities and deny us psychological growth.

No two people look at anything or anyone the same. When we look at something, we are not seeing it for what it is, we are seeing it for what we want it to be. The truth is, we may be looking at something or someone at that moment in time, but we are bringing our entire life experience and baggage to that circumstance. Perceptions are extremely dangerous: they lead to quick judgments, the refusal to look at facts and evidence, the inability to listen to other people, and inflexibility in changing our minds.

Example: Two prominent celebrities are perfect examples of this: Bill Cosby and Howard Stern. The perception of Bill Cosby, that he carefully crafted over fifty years, is one of a great family man, who is kind and generous, and whose life is built on the foundation of morals, values, and family. The image of Howard Stern, who has been in the entertainment industry for almost four decades, is someone who lacks morality, a soulless deviant who represents the worst of society and is a philandering adolescent. The public perception of these individuals couldn't be further from the truth of who they are reported to be in private.

During college, I worked at Blossom Music Center, a prestigious amphitheater in northeast Ohio. My two best friends, Barry and Craig, worked with me, and we worked almost every single event. Out of the hundreds of acts that we saw, one that always resonated with me was Bill Cosby. Cosby came to Blossom at the height of his entertainment and comedic fame. His entire act was centered around the love he had for his wife and family. Every comedian carefully crafts and hones his act with the sole purpose of engaging the audience and generating revenue. During his act, Cosby referenced his wife by name, Camille, and his children so many times that it was difficult to count. At the time, this was something that I accepted as fact and bought into, hook, line, and sinker, which is exactly what Cosby and his management team intended. Over the last twenty plus years, I have been a consistent Howard Stern listener. On his show, he has had breast examinations, anal ring tossing, mother-daughter sex acts, and every other type of entertainment act that many, if not most, people would consider obscene, inappropriate, and borderline pornographic.

Both individuals were perpetrating an entertainment fraud solely to amass immense wealth and fame. Howard Stern created a persona that would attract a worldwide fan base as well as the ire and disdain of millions, while Bill Cosby's professional misrepresentation had the entire world admiring and applauding his every move.

In recent years, we've come to realize that both men are opposites of the images they spent decades carefully crafting. Howard Stern has been reputed to never have cheated on his spouse, is a documented homebody, and lives a life contrary to the image he created. In contrast, Bill Cosby created a perception of morality that throughout his entire career was contradicted by the way he lived his private life. He turned out to be a serial rapist and philanderer. Both men have financially benefited and personally suffered from the perceptions that they have created. They have amassed a reported net worth of close to a billion dollars based on these inaccurate representations. These fraudulent perceptions are so ingrained that many people refuse to accept any fact to the contrary.

Lesson learned: Perceptions are not based on what we see, they are based on what we want to see, and more importantly, what we refuse to see. Perceptions cause us to inaccurately assess situations, relationships, and people, leading us down the path of illusion, not reality. Once a perception has been built in our mind, no fact or piece of evidence to the contrary will penetrate its exterior.

CHAPTER TWENTY-SIX

Drugs and Laws

There is not one law that is governed by this society that is not steeped in hypocrisy. We can't drink alcohol until we are 21, but we can fight and die for our country at 18. If the stipulation is that someone cannot drink until a certain age, isn't that an acknowledgment that alcohol is a drug and therefore should be considered dangerous? If a drug is dangerous, why is it permitted at any age and at any dosage? The answer is simple, because the government wants to espouse alcohol as being less dangerous than any other drug, so they can benefit from the billions of dollars of revenue that alcohol sales create. The government determines the legality or illegality of specific drugs, not based on the level of damage that they do to an individual or society but based on society's moral acceptance of certain drugs. Morally, alcohol is viewed differently than cocaine, therefore alcohol is accepted by society as legal and cocaine is not, although more people die yearly of alcohol abuse than they do of cocaine overdoses. Once the government realizes that society will accept the fraud they are perpetrating, that fraud becomes law. This is simply a matter of dollars and sense. Once the government can convince society that something makes sense, they can start lining their pockets with dollars. The only time the public doesn't factor into the equation is when legalizing a drug is costing the government dollars and cents.

Marijuana is a perfect example of this. The reason the government tells us that marijuana is illegal is that they deem it harmful and detrimental. In direct contrast, many studies show that marijuana alleviates numerous physical and emotional ailments as well as avoiding the metabolic damage that many pharmaceutical drugs cause. The reason it is illegal is that the government is in business with the medical community and the pharmaceutical industry, and legalizing marijuana would cost these parties billions of dollars in revenue. In my opinion, the government is concerned about their financial benefit, even to the physical and emotional detriment of society. Laws are not created for the benefit of society, they are created for the benefit of the people instituting them. In most cases, these laws are personally, physically, and financially detrimental to society. The bottom line with the government *is* always the bottom line. Anything that negatively affects the bottom line is met with immediate resistance. Anything that enhances the bottom line is met with open arms. Narcotics is the perfect example of this.

Example #1: Drug-dealers. Drug dealers are viewed as disreputable thugs, and often cold-blooded killers. We fail to acknowledge that we interact with these people daily: they're called pharmacists. The only difference between the two is the perception that the government has created, and that we have accepted and embraced as a society. Even the entertainment industry has perpetuated this perception. In the movies, drug dealers always wear black, which is perceived as evil, work at night, and are portrayed as shady, money-hungry, soulless individuals. Pharmacists wear white coats, work behind a counter, and greet you with a hello and a smile. They work bankers' hours and are considered your neighborhood friend who you can entrust with your health and the health of your family.

In the old westerns, the bad guy wears the black hat, is immersed in black attire and intends to do harm to anyone in his path, while the hero is dressed from head to toe in white and always finds a way to save the day. This doesn't just pertain to westerns, this has infiltrated every movie genre. In Star Wars, the stormtroopers wear spotless white uniforms and Darth Vader is encased in black.

This portrayal is intentional and has seeped into the psyche of society, pushing people away from drug dealers and towards legalized drugs with the sole purpose of funneling money towards the people in power.

Example #2: The National Football League (NFL). The NFL refuses to legalize marijuana for medicinal purposes to alleviate their players' pain. This isn't done because marijuana is harmful, it's done because the NFL, like the government, is in bed with the medical community and the pharmaceutical representatives who provide them with millions of dollars of revenue each year through marketing and advertising. They constantly espouse that their only concern is the safety and health of their players. At the same time, they are funneling every drug imaginable down the throats of their players, destroying their kidneys, livers, and every other organ in their systems. They even go out of their way to deny their players who play in states where marijuana is legalized. Hundreds of players have gone public stating that when they take marijuana, two extreme results occur. The first is that their pain decreases to the point where it almost becomes unnoticeable, and the second is when they take marijuana and quit using the legalized medicine that is forced upon them, they feel an astronomical difference in how their metabolic systems function. If the NFL listened to their players, it would cost them millions of dollars; therefore, they have no interest in listening to their players, as their sole purpose is to monetarily benefit from the companies whose drugs are damaging their athletes.

Lesson learned: The government is monetarily vested in keeping society sick and suppressed. The health of society could be remedied to a significant degree if the government's focus shifted from filling their pockets to the betterment of the people they were elected to protect. The cause and effect of this issue are simple: the cause of legalizing a drug that is less harmful than cigarettes, alcohol, and many drugs on the planet will affect the government's bottom line. Government is big business, and like any business, it's based on revenue. The only difference is the government does not have to wait for the customer to come to them, they bring their extortion to us.

CHAPTER TWENTY-SEVEN

The Price of Profit

The goal of every company is not just to attain your business, it is to ensure repeat business. Businesses accomplish this by making inferior products. Not every product made incorrectly is made that way because the manufacturer is incompetent, it is often by design. The higher quality the product, the less likely they are to attain repeat business.

Logic would mandate that if you do something correctly the first time, you won't need to do it again. For businesses, this is a recipe for disaster. If businesses worked under this premise, they would never have reoccurring customers; therefore, they would be out of business. We can send a man to the moon, but we can't put metal in a microwave. We have Lasik surgery, which can completely correct someone's eyesight within minutes, but we can't create a remedy for the common cold.

Many people believe that society's problems are beyond repair. I fundamentally disagree with that premise. It's not that these things cannot be repaired, it's that the people in power do not want them repaired, because repairing them would have long-lasting financial ramifications.

Example #1 Our government is the biggest culprit when it comes to mismanaging our money. It's not a coincidence that they are the middle man when it comes to dispersing our tax dollars. If the government allowed people to directly pay their taxes to an appropriate venue, then they would not be able to misappropriate our funds. Many people believe that cures for cancer and other diseases already exist. If these cures exist, there must be a reason they have not been disclosed. The reason these cures are not disclosed is that it would result in the loss of the billions of dollars for funding and research that the government generates annually.

Example #2 Technology: The instant we buy a new device, it is already obsolete. This isn't because companies keep perfecting technology at an earth-shattering pace. It's because they are withholding that technology and dispensing it at a pace where they can continually reap financial benefits. The more a business benefits a customer, the less the company benefits. Almost every dollar that we spend is not a dollar that we want to spend, it is a dollar we are forced to spend. We spend hundreds of millions of dollars a year, replacing things that were intentionally designed to malfunction and to become obsolete.

Example #3: In the movie, *Tucker, a Man and His Dreams*, the lead role of Preston Tucker is portrayed by Jeff Bridges. Tucker created an automobile in the late 1940s called "The Tucker," which rendered every automobile made by the Big Three: Ford Motor, Chrysler, and General Motors, obsolete. The minute the Big Three caught wind of Tucker's creation, their thought process should have been to immediately go back to the drawing board and create a better automobile. Instead, they combined their resources and united in discrediting Tucker, knowing if they discredited him, it would bury his creation. In hindsight, many people believe that Tucker's creation was not innovative or ahead of its time. Historians believe "The Tucker" was an automobile that already had been designed by one or more of the Big Three, but that they refused to bring it to market, knowing that the car of the future would result in their businesses suffering astronomical financial losses.

Lesson learned: The foundation of our country is money. When businesses are creating a product, when pharmaceutical companies and the government are thinking about disclosing a cure, and when technology is thinking of unveiling a new product, their thought processes are not focused on the money they are going to make, they are focused on the money they are going to lose.

CHAPTER TWENTY-EIGHT

Hiding Behind Our Masks

People have an innate desire to feel accepted. Beneath that desire is an intense fear of rejection. The people who ingrain the feeling of rejection in us are the same people who should be elevating our spirit. The punishments that we endure for not saying the things that people want us to say or doing the things they want us to do, cause us to change what we say and who we are. This conditions us to put on masks, causing us to create a persona that does not reflect our true selves. In battle, people suit up to protect themselves from an oncoming invasion. This is something that we do to protect ourselves from people daily. These masks protect us but create long-term damage, allowing people to see us as they want, but causing us to lose sight of who we are. The times that people are most upset with us coincide with the times we are not wearing any masks. People's opinion and perception of us changes depending on whether we are wearing the mask or not. The decision comes down to a simple choice: "Are we seeking external or internal comfort?" External comfort requires wearing the mask, internal comfort requires its removal. As adults, the decision is ours; as children, this decision is made for us. We had no control over the people who placed these masks on us, but we are in complete control of their removal. It is difficult for many to remove the mask because they've spent a lifetime interacting with people while wearing it. If taking off the mask feels insurmountable, start by eliminating the people that want you to wear it. The faster you eliminate these people, the easier it will become to remove the mask.

Example: I love cartoons, comics, and superheroes. They were an escape from an unhappy childhood. I admire the messages that these cartoons gave me. I love the inner conflict and duality that each super-hero deals with when they don their alter-ego disguise. My two favorites are Batman and Spiderman. I did not realize until later that my two favorites were the ones who wore masks. They originally wore these masks to conceal their identity from their enemies and to protect their loved ones from reprisal. As time went on, these masks and their alter ego caused an identity crisis between the superhero they were portraying and the mere mortals they were. They both started out wanting to uphold justice, to protect and defend the people who could not protect and defend themselves. What they never factored into the equation is that these masks would create an internal divide. Their initial concern was avoiding external detection, without realizing it would create internal conflict. I view superheroes the way society views law enforcement. Criminals don't respect the individual, they fear the uniform. Criminals didn't fear Bruce Wayne and Peter Parker, they feared Batman and Spiderman. Even with the purest of intentions, there was no way that Bruce Wayne and Peter Parker could deny the empowerment that came with donning their masks. Just like in society, when a law enforcement officer puts on his uniform. The masks that were originally put on to protect later became all-consuming and, when taken off, it became the equivalent of letting all the air out of a balloon. The masks that we put on were not to protect society and defend the defenseless; we put them on to protect ourselves because we were defenseless. The problem we face when we take these masks off is that it invokes other people to burst our balloons.

Lesson learned: We learn how easy it is to put on masks to protect ourselves from people who punish us for being who we are. Social media is a perfect example of this. Honesty on social media has destroyed many lives. Saying what you want to say through social media is very easy. It's the equivalent of taking off the mask. The difficulty of reversing the damage that occurs from being honest on social media is why society chooses to never remove the mask.

CHAPTER TWENTY-NINE

People's Disposition is Determined by Their Position

People's disposition is determined by their position, meaning when someone's position changes, their disposition changes. Human behavior is like simple math. You change the variable, you change the equation. People truly believe that they have a moral compass and a foundation that's based on values and unshakable character. The minute someone espouses themselves moral, I immediately become suspicious. Experience has taught me that people's morality is based on their position at that given moment. Money is a perfect example of this. When people attain wealth, their behavior often changes. When people's behavior changes based on their financial situation, others will say that the money changed them, and they often add, "Money is the root of all evil." This cliché is erroneous. The fraudulent personality is not the one that comes out when someone attains money, it's the disingenuous personality that existed before money factored into the equation. We spend a lifetime trying to attain wealth, contorting our personality in pursuit of it. Once we attain our own wealth, we don't have to bend for anyone.

From the outside, it appears that money brings out the worst in people. From the inside, it brings out who we really are. A large percentage of society is not in the financial position to represent who they truly are; hence, their disposition is determined by their position. Money is the greatest truth serum, one whiff of it and you cannot stop people from being who they are and saying what they feel.

Money is not the only reason we suppress our feelings and our true nature. We suppress our nature because in most circumstances, revealing our identity has severe consequences. This suppression occurs wherever we go. It starts the minute people and society punish us for being who we are. This suppression empowers the suppressor and creates internal conflict within us.

Example #1: As stated, money is the greatest truth serum. Right behind money is alcohol. Alcohol has become the built-in excuse for people to act or speak in a way that is reflective of who they are without reprisal. People look forward to getting drunk, knowing whatever they do and say will often be dismissed. Alcohol is to our suppression what anger is to Bruce Banner. The anger allows Bruce Banner to release the Incredible Hulk, the same as alcohol allows our inner beast to run wild.

Example #2: Many professional athletes come from modest means. When they acquire wealth for the first time, it gives them the opportunity to elevate themselves above the circumstances that they have known their entire life. They are in a societal position where everyone dreams of being. Once the athlete reaches this position, the people in their past try to pull them back. These people call the athlete a sell-out and a traitor, refusing to acknowledge that their words are rooted in jealousy. The athlete's position has changed, therefore his disposition changes. The people left behind who admonish the athlete are truly incensed that their position has not changed. Wealth gives people choices that were not available before they attained it, allowing them to change their disposition. When an athlete is drafted professionally, their financial situation isn't the only thing that changes. Every aspect of their life changes. This doesn't create a problem for the athlete, it creates a problem for everyone they know.

Michael Irvin, former Dallas Cowboys wide receiver and current Hall of Famer, was once asked in an interview, "What is the greatest thing about being drafted by the Dallas Cowboys?" Irvin, who played collegiately at the University of Miami, said the greatest thing about being drafted by Dallas was that it was 2,500 miles from his friends and family in Florida. He elaborated that the distance was so great that the people who were hitting him up for money were too cheap to buy a plane ticket to travel to get it. He also conveyed that these same people were calling him a sell-out and disloyal behind his back. The hypocrites judging him, while at that same time asking him for money, were expecting him to fly back to Florida to give it to them.

Example #3: Marriage. Couples often stay together because they do not have the resources to divorce. They lie to everyone, including themselves, as to why they stay together, saying that it's for the betterment of their children or that they believe in the institution in marriage, instead of acknowledging that they are not in the financial position to change their circumstances. The lies they create are said to ease their conscience when it only denies them the ability to individually move forward.

Lesson learned: Many people convey they are happy with their lives and the choices they have made, refusing to admit that a lack of wealth has made life's choices for them. Hypocrisy occurs when we criticize someone for doing something that we would do ourselves if we were in their position. We believe our judgments of other people are based on who they are; the truth is, they are often based on who we are not, and the decisions we make in life are not rooted in money, they are rooted in the lack of it.

CHAPTER THIRTY

Accountability

L ife is full of contradictions, with accountability being at the top of the list. Lack of accountability is at the root of society's problems. Personal accountability has been a flaw of mine as well. We demand that people take ownership of their mistakes when we never do, and we hold them to a standard that we never attain. This character flaw is not mutually exclusive to the people entrusted with our upbringing, it is a societal flaw. As I have aged, I view myself and society as a funnel, becoming more narrow-minded and less accountable as we get older. Accountability, like many characteristics, is something that is educated out of us by society. We grow up having authority figures verbalize how important it is to be accountable while watching them avoid accountability and consequences by dispensing blame on everyone but themselves.

I love the human condition. People will exhaust every option to avoid taking accountability because subconsciously they know that if they take accountability, they must change their situation instead of someone or something changing it for them. Accountability is the last step before action, which is one of the reasons people avoid it.

Example #1: When I owned my fitness center, one of my listed rules was that no one under the age of 14 was permitted. I did this solely for liability reasons because my first and main concern was to protect myself and my business. I had a nutritional center where members could sit down, have a smoothie, and watch a movie. One day a member knocked on my door and I could see that she was physically upset. She conveyed to me that I needed to change the movie because it was too violent for her foster son. The movie was *The Godfather*, and when I walked out, her foster son was sitting at the counter. I could see the boy was under the age of fourteen. She looked at me and said, "Are you going to change the movie?" Even though she verbalized it in question form, she was giving me a command. I told her the problem wasn't the movie, the problem was that she hadn't read the rules and regulations posted on my front door, which stated, "No one under the age of 14 is allowed beyond this point." She read this, then proceeded to follow me to my office, telling me that she had just gone through a nasty divorce and that her husband had gained sole custody of their two children, which was why she was fostering the young boy. She assumed her explanation would garner her special treatment. I told her that her circumstance did not supersede my liability and that the boy would have to leave the premises. Not liking my answer and refusing to take accountability, she walked out of my office and started complaining to fellow members about me.

Within ten to fifteen minutes, four members entered my office. They were two couples: one a lawyer and his wife, the other a doctor and his wife. This wasn't a coincidence, these being members who assumed their professions and positions in the community would have influence over me. They came in "guns blazing," telling me I was being unfair and insensitive, refusing to acknowledge the woman's personal situation. Fighting fire with fire, I chose to hold them accountable to their positions in the community. I reached into my cabinet and pulled out two contracts. Before I discussed the contracts, I asked them to reiterate their positions. They explained that as the owner of the gym, I shouldn't be so rigid, and that life was about relationships, not liability. I handed each man a contract and told them, you're correct, life is about relationships, not just money and liability. I instructed the attorney to write in legalese that I would allow the child access to my facility if they would assume complete legal and medical liability for him. The wife of the doctor became upset. She told me it wasn't their responsibility to assume liability for my business. I replied by saying that her husband told me life is about relationships, and since you have a relationship with the woman that far supersedes mine, I was going to hold them accountable for that relationship. She replied again, your business isn't our responsibility. I responded by stating that she was correct, my business was not their responsibility, therefore their opinions about how I should run it were not their business. The doctor and the lawyer looked at each other, stood up, and along with their wives left my office, never discussing this issue with me again.

All I had to do to resolve the problem was to hold them to the same level of accountability that they were trying to hold me to. This demand of accountability led to a positive action, which is not always the case.

Example #2: The O.J. Simpson trial brings this reality front and center. During the trial, I watched an interview with Denise Brown, Nicole's sister. The entire interview was based around a conversation they had. Nicole told her sister that she was going to leave O.J. and was going to take full accountability for staying in an abusive relationship. Nicole added that the happiness and safety of her children were paramount. During this conversation, Nicole presented Denise with every document and photo related to O.J.'s physical abuse. Denise asked Nicole why she was giving these documents to her, to which Nicole replied, "Now that I've taken accountability and am going to take action, I want you to have these things for the record because once I take action, O. J's going to kill me." Within weeks of their conversation, they attended a recital for Nicole's daughter which O.J. also attended. After the recital, Nicole and her family went to a local restaurant to celebrate and Nicole told O.J. that he was not invited. That was the night that she and Ron Goldman were murdered. Nicole's taking accountability for her life and holding O.J. accountable for his actions was a brave and admirable stand, tragically, it was her last.

Lessons learned: The one characteristic that most people share is lack of accountability. The more we try to enforce accountability on someone, the more resistant they become. Our lack of accountability is at the heart of all our problems. Personal growth and development cannot occur without accountability. This lack of accountability may create a short-term reprieve, but it denies long-term growth.

CHAPTER THIRTY-ONE

Societal Versus Personal Accountability

We're a society that demands accountability from its individuals but doesn't offer it to them. Many of the problems that occur in society could be stopped or lessened if the people responsible for protecting us took accountability. Laziness breeds a lack of accountability, a lack of accountability breeds a lack of action, a lack of action can lead to catastrophic results. In a scenario with multiple individuals who are involved, there is often accountability or blame to be equally dispensed.

Example #1: In an earlier chapter, we talked about the serial killer Ted Bundy. Before Bundy's last killing spree in Florida, he was incarcerated in a Colorado jail. He was confined to a cell that had an overhead airshaft above his ceiling's light fixture. He removed this light fixture, propelled himself into the airshaft, and escaped unnoticed. That was the second time Bundy escaped from prison. The first time Bundy escaped, he was left unattended in the prison library, seated next to an open window. After his second escape, he stole a car and drove to Florida. While in Florida, he broke into a sorority house and an off-campus home, killing two women. The following day, he followed a twelve-year-old girl leaving school and murdered her. Bundy was accused and convicted of these murders and died by electrocution. (Nordheimer, 1989).

In my opinion, Bundy committed the murders, but the correctional officers who allowed him to escape were just as accountable. During recorded interviews, it has become public record that two weeks before Bundy escaped for the second time, inmates told multiple correctional officers that they could hear him in the airshaft above their cells. Bundy was obviously trying to find the perfect escape route. Bundy was aware that he was trying to escape, other inmates were aware that he was trying to escape, and law enforcement officers were aware that he was trying to escape, which leads to the question: how was he able to escape? The answer is simple, a lack of accountability by the law enforcement officers to take the information they were given seriously. Their job was to protect society from the individuals who were housed in their prison, not to ignore credible information that could have prevented one of the world's worst serial killers from murdering again. These correctional officers were just as culpable as Bundy and should have faced the same criminal charges and consequences. Refusing to accept the information they were given as credible makes them all accessories before the fact. Numerous women were murdered solely based on correctional officers allowing a serial killer to escape.

Example #2: Serial killer Jeffrey Dahmer. Dahmer killed, dismembered, sexually violated, and disposed of his victims. Dahmer faced numerous life sentences without the option of parole and was killed in prison at the hands of other inmates. He should not have faced these life sentences alone. Again, law enforcement officers are equally responsible for many of these murders. While living in Milwaukee, one of Dahmer's victims, a thirteen-year-old Vietnamese boy, escaped his clutches. An individual saw this boy running down the street naked and bleeding from his anus. This individual called 911, and law enforcement officers were dispatched. Officers found the boy, put him in the back of the squad car, and tried to ascertain as much information as possible. The boy didn't speak English, was completely disoriented, and freezing from the fact that he was naked and had been running down the street in the middle of winter. The officers assumed the boy was homosexual because of the bleeding from his anus, therefore, they refused to take him back to the station and acquire an interpreter. Instead, they drove him back to Dahmer's apartment after obtaining Dahmer's physical address during the boy's questioning. The boy quickly paid the ultimate price of the officer's negligence and lack of accountability.

This boy was victim number eleven out of fifteen victims (Mirror, 1991). This boy's life and the lives of future victims could have been saved if the people entrusted to protect society had been accountable to the position they held.

Lesson learned: Society puts people in a position to judge individuals' accountability, or lack of it, daily. Government officials, judges, and police officers all swear oaths to adhere to a higher standard. Imagine where society would be if an accountability clause was added to the oath these individuals take.

CHAPTER THIRTY-TWO

The Name Game

Words are the world's most powerful weapon. Once people in positions of power learned this inevitable fact, guilt, manipulation, and suppression became the order of the day. The twisting of words to suit an individuals' purpose has caused many people to suffer severe psychological and emotional harm.

Example #1: Among the many words that have been attributed to me, 'selfish' is at the top of the list. Whenever I am called selfish, narcissistic, uncaring, dishonest, or any other word that society deems unflattering, it always is conveyed in a negative tone. I quickly learned that whenever those words were applied to me, it was immediately after someone was not getting what they wanted from me. I looked up these words in a dictionary, wanting to see the definitions of the words people were using to define me. I quickly realized that the words were not as negative as they were portrayed to be. Wanting to balance out my thought process, I started making a mental checklist every time someone said something to me that would be perceived as positive. These positive responses occurred every time I did or said something that someone wanted me to do or say. This taught me that people's opinions of me were not based on who I was or what I believed in, they were based on who they wanted me to be and what they wanted me to say. People's opinions of us are anchored in our thoughts and their thoughts being aligned. The minute our opinions are not the same as theirs, we no longer coincide with them. This is an ultimate life lesson. People know exactly what they are doing when they use words to paint us in a negative light. They realize these words will cause us to alter our behavior, aligning it with the behavior they want from us.

Example #2: Wordplay is the foundation that interconnects society, the mortar to our bricks. We do not view people based on the things that they say, we view them based on the things we want to hear. Marketing and advertising companies understand this principle better than anyone. This understanding allows them to manipulate words for their financial benefit. When we hear the word *doctor*, many people think caring, compassionate, and concerned about their patient's well-being. When we hear the word *lawyer*, many people think unethical, scheming, and disreputable. Professionally, there is little difference between the two, other than our perceptions. They both charge for a service with no guarantee of the outcome.

Wordplay is the reason society views these two professions so differently. Doctors call the people who come to see them 'patients,' which has a warm, fuzzy, caring, heartfelt connotation to it. Lawyers call the people who come to see them 'clients,' which has a cold, calculated, and impersonal connotation. Society's perception of these professions is based on doctors having a much better marketing and advertising campaign behind them. By the changing of one-word hundreds of years ago, we now perceive both professions differently. It's much easier to monetize a 'patient' than a 'client.' Once you create an environment that's conducive to the perception of caring, it becomes much easier to monetarily extract from people.

Words are amazing. The minute you can get someone to hear what they want, you can steer them in any direction you choose. This wordplay exists unilaterally. For example, cars are no longer used, they're 'certified pre-owned.' Television shows are no longer new, they're 'all new.' Appliances are no longer new, they're 'brand new.' Groceries are no longer fresh, they're 'daily fresh.' Wordplay is not just used to extract money, it's used to extract information. When we call a business, their recording often states, "This call may be monitored or recorded for quality assurance purposes." This is a lie, it's being recorded for legal purposes. The business knows their recording is disingenuous, they are also aware that if they disclose that it's for liability purposes, the customer will immediately terminate the phone call.

Example #3: Companies enhance verbal misrepresentations with visual misrepresentations. Grocery stores enlarge every item. Every beer manufacturer shows beautiful people with perfectly chiseled bodies drinking their product. No parent can hear the word Michelin without seeing an infant sitting in their tires. The implication is, if you care about your child, you'll buy their product. There isn't one product sold on television that doesn't misrepresent or falsely advertise. It has become so commonplace that we're oblivious to it.

Lesson learned: Our world is built on lies, misrepresentations, wordplay, deception, and fraud. We have changed the meaning of every word or image to suit our purpose, using them to manipulate people to the point where they expect and often demand that we manipulate them. We use words and images to bend people to our will, and to suppress them, all for our personal or financial enrichment. Once we understand this fundamental premise, then we can no longer blame people or society for manipulating and coercing us. The hypocrisy of this lesson is that we do this daily but despise when it is done to us.

CHAPTER THIRTY-THREE

Fraud

The term 'fraud' has negative personal and legal ramifications. The dictionary lists fraud as 'trickery.' By that definition, every person on the planet has committed fraud. Fraud is a matter of perspective, and often when people are defrauded, they look for legal recourse and monetary restitution. Many believe the reason they are filing a lawsuit is that what has been done to them is wrong, but, it's often because the person who defrauded them was better than they were at defrauding.

Example #1: When a person is offered four hundred acres of prime real estate in Boca Raton, Florida for $40,000, they should immediately become suspicious. Once they realize the $40,000 they spent bought them an acre of swampland in the Everglades, they scream fraud. These people portray themselves as victims and seek legal recourse. The truth is, anyone who expects to get 400 hundred acres in Boca Raton, FL for $40,000 is delusional. We are so focused on taking advantage of people that we are oblivious to when it's being done to us. What people are often upset about is that the person they were trying to take advantage of took advantage of them. This ties into the earlier chapter that our disposition is based on our position.

Example #2: It is illegal to misrepresent a product, its price, and its life expectancy. When a product doesn't live up to the advertisement, we call that fraud. We never scream fraud when the product supersedes the advertisement. When we are on the positive side of false advertising, we never complain, it's only when we're on the negative side that we scream fraud. If it was an ethical dilemma, then we would be giving money back every time a product exceeded its advertised value. Fraud often comes down to human nature and self-benefit. The music industry is an example of this.

Example #3: I have a Rolling Stones Farewell Tour T-shirt. I believe the date on the shirt is 1987. Thirty-plus years later, the Rolling Stones are still on their farewell tour. This is the ultimate definition of fraud. In representing it as a "Farewell Tour," every band can charge astronomical prices, knowing their fans will want to see their final performance. This fraud has become socially accepted, therefore it's not even viewed as fraud. If we love the concert and enjoy the show, we forget about the indiscretion. The saying, "You get what you paid for," shouldn't cause us to overlook intentional deception. Fraud is subjective and often is determined by whether we benefit from someone, or they benefited from us.

Lesson learned: When we benefit from someone or something, we never give it a second thought. When we are on the wrong end of the benefit, fraud factors into the equation. In many circumstances, the issue isn't fraud, it's our lack of objectivity in how we perceive what's being done to us and, more importantly, what we're doing to others.

CHAPTER THIRTY-FOUR

Do as I Say, Not as I Do

W e live in a society where no one's actions match their words. This conflict creates an inner divide at an age when we can't understand it. We've all heard the cliché 'actions speak louder than words.' We've become a society that values words over actions. Many adults understand this, which allows them to tell us one thing and do another. What they don't realize is the damage they cause when children see their actions contradict their words. People believe if they tell us something enough, we'll overlook what they're showing us. Adults don't realize that we often quit listening to them the minute their actions contradict their words.

Example #1: Courtroom dramas are one of my favorite movie genres. At some point, testimony or evidence is presented that the jury should not have heard or seen. Once the judge realizes they made an error, they will instruct the jury to disregard it. This is impossible. It's the equivalent of putting the toothpaste back in the tube or the genie back in the bottle. In life, once someone shows us evidence of their character, and their words contradict that evidence, we cannot retroactively go back and disregard everything we have seen. We have all worked at a job where a superior directly defined our responsibilities. We learn that supervisors have different job requirements for people who are in their good graces. I have never worked for a company where the supervisor lived up to the rules they were conveying to me.

Example #2: In college, I worked at the Richfield Coliseum, an indoor entertainment venue in Richfield, Ohio. I worked security just as I had at Blossom Music Center. Several supervisors worked at both venues. During one event, I worked the elevator on the lower level concourse at a Cleveland Cavaliers game. My job description, which was stated numerous times, was to never leave my post. About 50 feet from where I stood was a room where the Cavaliers' wives stayed during the game. During that game, two teenagers ran out of the elevator towards the court. Before they got to the court, I caught one of them and courtside security caught the other. If I had not caught the individual, he would have run right onto the court during the game. Unbeknownst to me, this was a ploy, as there was a third person in the elevator who I didn't see. That teenager waited until I chased his two friends, then ran into the room designated for the Cavaliers' wives and proceeded to flip over the buffet table and trash the room. After the game, my supervisor called me into his office to inform me that I was being suspended. He asked me if I knew why, and I responded that it was because he did not like me. He then stated, "No, Harry, it's because you left your post, which is a violation of your job responsibility." I asked, "What would have happened if I stayed at my post, followed my job description to the letter of the law, had not chased down the individual, and allowed him to get on the court?" He explained that I would not have been suspended because I would have done my job the way he had expressed it to me, which was very convenient for him to say but was something we both knew was not true. He reached into his drawer, pulled out a suspension notice, and asked me if I had anything else to say while he was filling it out. I replied that I had nothing else to say, but that I needed to go to the locker room and get something and would be right back. He said that would not be a problem. I ran to the locker room, grabbed my friends, Nate and Steve, and said, "I need your help." Without hesitation, they followed me back to the supervisor's office. My supervisor asked, "Why are Nate and Steve here, they have nothing to do with this." I then informed him that they had everything to do with it. Two weeks earlier, Nate and Steve faced a similar situation. Not only were they not suspended for it, they received accommodations. The supervisor refused to look at Nate and Steve and focused his attention on me, realizing that he had given them letters of accommodation for doing the exact same thing he was about to hand me a letter of suspension for. I said, "if it wasn't personal, and we all disobeyed his verbal command, then why the two different results?" Like most people, he started to look for a way out of the situation when there wasn't one. My goal here was to show two identical situations to avoid being suspended, which is exactly what occurred.

Lesson learned: When people tell you, "Do as I say, not as I do," but then also tell you, "Actions speak louder than words," it creates a lifetime of indecision, self-doubt, and detrimental behavior. We must force ourselves to pick a side: are we going to believe people based on what we see from them, or are we going to believe people based on what they tell us? That decision will allow us to be free of the conflict within ourselves that other people have spent a lifetime creating.

CHAPTER THIRTY-FIVE

Flip the Script

The reason other people take advantage of us is that we have conditioned them to do so. Oftentimes, people treat us like blood to a shark: once they get the scent, they go in for the kill. We give off numerous scents: fear, insecurity, paranoia, desperation, panic, and not wanting to be perceived poorly. These are attributes that cause people to invade our space and attempt to extract what they want out of us. All it takes to reverse this trend is altering the way we normally act and respond to people. This change doesn't have to occur all at once, it can occur incrementally, one step at a time. When we quit worrying about how people perceive us, what they think of us, whether they approve of us, and if they will be upset or disappointed with us, then we have a great chance of flipping the script and turning what was once our weakness into our strength. If we videotaped ourselves, we would be appalled by how many times we acquiesce to other people's demands, simply because we lack the courage to stand our ground. Years of conditioning, suppression, manipulation, and control have ingrained these characteristics in us. We had no control over being suppressed, but we are in complete control of overcoming the suppression. The process is simplistic: whenever you leave an encounter, ask yourself one simple question, "Did I act and speak in a way that is truly reflective of how I think and feel?"

If the answer is 'yes,' then you are being true to who you are.

Life is unfair. Two sides rarely leave an encounter mutually benefited. It's the equivalent of a game ending in a tie. It rarely, if ever, happens, and when it does, neither side is satisfied. What you must determine is whether you want to appease other people at your own detriment, or if you want to be true to who you are, which means upsetting the status quo. The minute you become comfortable with other people's disapproval is the minute you go from prey to predator, allowing you to flip the script in most situations. Once you learn not to allow people to take advantage of you, it becomes liberating and empowering and will energize you until your next encounter.

Example: My doctor's office was five minutes from my health club. During one visit, I was taken back to see the doctor two hours past my scheduled time. This situation is not unique to me, every person knows what it feels like to wait for hours on end to see their doctor. The two-hour delay and a ninety-minute consultation and examination cost me an entire afternoon away from my business. After the examination, I went to the front desk to pay my bill. My co-pay was $45. When I pulled out my checkbook, the receptionist told me to make it for $90. When I asked why, she explained to me that when I came to the office the previous week for my preliminary appointment, I was an hour late. Despite being an hour late, it didn't throw off the doctor's schedule because I still waited another hour before being seen. I asked her why it matter how late I was if he still saw me two hours past my designated time. She replied that it doesn't matter when he sees you, we charge based on your appointment time. Instead of arguing, I just continued to ask questions for the sole purpose of getting her to state their position.

The first mistake in conflict is that we want to talk instead of listening, and we become emotional instead of logical. We'll never understand someone's position until we give them the opportunity to state

THE TRUTH IS A LIE

it. I asked her if she viewed the doctor's time as more valuable than the patients. She replied, "No." I then asked what is the point of having a designated scheduled time when the doctor never honors it? I told her "In two years, he's never taken me at my scheduled time, therefore, I saw no problem in being late because what they consider an hour late, I consider valuable time that could be spent at my business. She replied that she understood, but that's how they conduct business. I replied, "How would you like to pay me?" She asked, "What do you mean, pay you?" I responded, "You stated that the doctor viewed the patient's time as just as valuable as his own. If that's true and he charges $45 per hour when a patient is past his/her appointment time, then they have to compensate the patient when the patient is on time and the doctor is hours past his scheduled appointment time." I proceeded to tell her that I charge $75 per hour for personal training and that each time I must wait for the doctor, it's costing me money. And when I'm late, it doesn't cost him a penny. I elaborated, telling her that if what she said was true, and they view the patient's time as equal to the doctor's, then compensation must go both ways.

In that instant, based on her words and locking herself into a position, I was able to flip the script. She went from asking to answering questions. She went from a position of power to a position that allowed her no flexibility. I told her that without patients, the doctor has no practice, and if they truly value their patients, they wouldn't make them wait for one second past their scheduled time. I finished by saying that I appreciated her telling me that they value their patients and they consider them just as important, if not more, than the doctor. I then asked her if she would like to pay me by check or cash. Realizing she was in a bad position, she asked me to come around back and have a seat, so we could discuss it in detail. Realizing that she didn't want this conversation overheard by the other patients, I replied, "No, I want to be paid now." She replied, "There'll be no charge for your co-pay and there'll be no charge for your co-pay moving forward." I replied, "Have a nice day."

Lesson learned: If you can take all the suppression and manipulation that you have endured and learn from it, you can often use it to your advantage. The most valuable lessons we learn are often the ones that are initially the most painful. When we feel pain, we become emotional instead of absorbing it and using it as fuel to drive us. Once you learn to embrace it and use it constructively, you will start living in a manner that's reflective of who you really are. If we learn to listen and apply logic instead of emotion, we will be able to flip the script in most situations.

EPILOGUE

This book lays a foundation based on control, manipulation, and human nature and behavior. This foundation will give you the ability to understand what has been done to you and why. The next series of books will build upon that foundation and give you a solid idea of how to overcome these issues so that you can leave them where they belong: in your past.

BIBLIOGRAPHY

"Heads in the freezer horror of America's CANNIBAL PSYCHOPATH; Without a doubt the most reviled serial killer of modern times, Jeffrey Dahmer ate victims' flesh for thrills - and planned to furnish a room with body trophies." *Mirror* [London, England] 29 Jan. 2011: 4. *Business Insights: Global.* http://bi.gale-group.com.ezproxy.snhu.edu/global/article/GALE%7CA247800153?u=nhc_main&sid=ebsco. Accessed 21 Aug. 2018.

Jennings, F. (1994). Reviews -- American Holocaust: Columbus and the Conquest of the New World by David E. Stannard. *Early American Literature, 29*(3), 305. Retrieved from http://ezproxy.snhu.edu/login?url=https://search-proquest-com.ezproxy.snhu.edu/docview/215383939?accountid=3783

Nordheimer, Jon. "Bundy Is Put to Death in Florida After Admitting Trail of Killings." *New York Times*, 25 Jan. 1989. *Opposing Viewpoints in Context*, http://link.gale-group.com.ezproxy.snhu.edu/apps/doc/A175611228/OVIC?u=nhc_main&sid=OVIC&xid=7420919c. Accessed 21 Aug. 2018.

Selfish. 2018. In *Merriam-Webster.com.*
Retrieved September 7, 2018, from https://www.merriam-webster.com/dictionary/selfish

Tzu, S. (2012). *The Art of War*. L. Giles. (Ed.). Retrieved from Amazon.com

Vanorman, A. and Jarosz, B. (2016). *Suicide Replaces Homicide as Second-Leadning Cause of Death Among U.S. Teenagers.* Population Reference Bureau. Retrieved September 26, 2018: https://www.prb.org/suicide-replaces-homicide-second-leading-cause-death-among-us-teens/

Wilson, P. K. (2018). *Encyclopedia Britannica*. Sherlock Holmes. Retrieved September 26, 2018: https://www.britannica.com/topic/Sherlock-Holmes

Made in the USA
Las Vegas, NV
21 December 2020

14476008R00069